From the Sin-é Café to the Black Hills

Books of poetry by the same author

Iron Mountain Road

Dyckman-200th Street

From the Sin-é Café to the Black Hills

NOTES ON THE NEW IRISH

Eamonn Wall

THE UNIVERSITY OF WISCONSIN PRESS

The University of Wisconsin Press
2537 Daniels Street
Madison, Wisconsin 53718

3 Henrietta Street
London WC2E 8LU, England

1   3   5   4   2

Printed in the United States of America

Some of the chapters in this book originally appeared in the following publications: *Colby Quarterly* 34, no. 4 (Dec. 1998), 303–14: "'Even Better Than the Real Thing': Brian Moore's *The Great Victorian Collection*"; *Critique: Studies in Contemporary Fiction* 40, no. 4 (Summer 1999), 355–63: "The Long Journey Home to Brooklyn: Michael Stephens's *Books of the Dead*"; *Éire-Ireland* 30, no. 4 (Winter 1996), 7–17: "Exile, Attitude, and the Sin-é Café: Notes on the New Irish"; *Forkroads: A Journal of Ethnic-American Literature* 1, no. 4 (Summer 1996), 66–75: "Irish Voices, American Writing, and Green Cards"; *Nua: Studies in Contemporary Irish Writing* 1, no. 2 (Spring 1998), 1–16: "The Search for Majestic Shades: Contemporary American Poets Migrate to Ireland"; *New Hibernia Review* 2, no. 4 (Winter 1998), 9–23: "The Black Hills, the Gorey Road, and Eavan Boland's *Object Lessons*"; and *Five Fingers Review* (forthcoming): "Immigration, Technology, and Sense of Place." "Four Paintings by Danny Maloney" was published in the anthology *Ireland in Exile: Irish Writers Abroad,* edited by Dermot Bolger (Dublin: New Island Books, 1993).

"Rockin' the Bronx" words and music by Larry Kirwan © 1993 EMI Blackwood Music Inc. and Starry Plough Music, all rights controlled and administered by EMI Blackwood Music Inc. All Rights Reserved. International Copyright Secured. Used by permission. "American Wake" words and music by Larry Kirwan © 1994 EMI Blackwood Music Inc. and Starry Plough Music, all rights controlled and administered by EMI Blackwood Music Inc. All rights Reserved. International Copyright Secured. Used by permission.

Library of Congress Cataloging-in-Publication Data

Wall, Eamonn, 1955–
From the Sin-é Café to the Black Hills: notes on the new Irish / Eamonn Wall.
154 pp.   cm.
ISBN 0-299-16720-8 (cloth: alk. paper)
ISBN 0-299-16724-0 (pbk.: alk. paper)
1. American literature—Irish American authors—History and criticism. 2. American literature—Ireland—History and criticism. 3. Irish Americans—Intellectual life. 4. Irish Americans in literature. 5. Irish Americans—Biography. 6. Immigrants in literature. 7. Ireland—In literature. 8. Wall, Eamonn, 1955–
I. Title.
PS153.I78 W35 1999
810.9'89162—dc21   99-6590

For Philip Casey

Born Irish, I observe the world through Irish sensibilities, take for granted an Irish way of doing things, am marked by small idiosyncrasies of behavior and accent, and am reminded of familiarities of early environment when I'm separated from them.

—William Trevor, *Excursions in the Real World*

Contents

Preface

This book represents a personal and literary exploration of the American landscape—books and rivers, mountains and streets, diverse peoples and the open road. It is the culmination of a project which grew out of opportunities to write two essays which would report on my own experiences as an immigrant and my engagement with my new home and its literature. The first, for Thomas Dillon Redshaw when he edited *Éire-Ireland*, set out to describe the attitudes of the "New Irish," the immigrants of my generation who arrived in the United States in the 1980s; the second, for David Kherdian's *Forkroads*, was an attempt to understand Irish America and its literature in relation to the Ireland in which I grew up. In both, I sought to understand the Irish diaspora—how the journey away from Ireland has altered attitude, identity, and sense of place, and how the recent Irish in America have fared in the melting pot. Also, I have searched for those aspects of the Irish way of life which have remained unaltered by the diaspora and which remind us of the extent to which Irish and Irish Americans share a common language. For this book, I have sought to expand on these themes, to explore complexities in more detail, to introduce some other aspects of the experience of diaspora which are important, and to locate points where the Irish and Irish American worlds converge and pull apart.

This is not a book of personal essays in the strictest sense. My own life in America has been ordinary enough in many respects, so a book based solely on personal experience would not make the most compelling of reading. It's not what I wished to write. Nor is this a book of literary criticism in the strictest sense, though many novels and poems are discussed and analyzed. To make issues of genre even more problematic, one can argue this is not a book of essays at all since it includes one piece of fiction. From my perspective though, this is the book I wanted to produce, as it is an attempt to lay side by side different aspects of my own life and voice, both of which have been transformed by time spent in the United States, and one which responds to the complex nature of my own experience. Also, I have sought to discover the best frameworks for particular theses and concerns, and this is why, for example, the essays on Michael Stephens and Brian Moore are examples of traditional literary criticism while those on Mary Gordon and Eavan Boland are not. When it came time to write of AIDS, I found fiction worked better than the essay. With respect to how this book has been shaped, I have been helped greatly by feminist literary criticism and by the advent of Cultural Studies, both of which have freed my mind, limited by a traditional literary education, and let the voice shape the book rather than the other way around.

Clearly, as an immigrant myself, it is impossible for me to write of the subject at a complete remove. However, the academic essay has offered me a kind of necessary distance from a subject. In this respect, my training as a scholar has been more useful than I ever thought it would be. At other points, aspects of the personal essay have been useful to me in framing this narrative; but even in those essays which will seem most personal, the reader will find absorption with writers and their books, which are the words and thoughts of those who have passed this way before me, and who have served as my teachers. Furthermore, what I have tried to do is write a book more full of personality than provenance. It will be clear to the reader that I am in no way attempting to write a canonical literary history of Irish America. Had I written this book fifteen years ago, the narrative would have been handled in a more traditional manner. But, I am no longer the person I was then: living in America, absence from Ireland, and becoming a parent have all combined to make me reject former notions of how books should be written. As a citizen of Ireland and a permanent resident of the United States who gets back to Ireland frequently, I am both hybrid immigrant and hybrid exile. My account is equally a hybrid one as this is what the voice demands.

I am very grateful to everyone who has helped me complete this project. At different stages in the process, a variety of people in the United States and Ireland have come to my aid—by providing hospitality and offering generous friendship and encouragement. I wish to acknowledge special debts to James Liddy and Jim Chapson in Milwaukee and Coolgreany; George O'Brien of Georgetown University; Thomas Dillon Redshaw and James Rogers of the Center for Irish Studies at the University of St. Thomas; Jeanne Flood of Wayne State University; David Gardiner of Milliken University; Charles Fanning of Southern Illinois University; Quitman Marshall and Lindsay O'Neil in Columbia, South Carolina; Conor

Howard, Elgy Gillespie, Aife Murray, Deborah Hunter McWilliams, and Stephen Arkin in California; Helena Mulkerns, Emer Martin, and Thomas McGonigle in New York; Greg Delanty in Vermont; David Kherdian in New York and California; Michael Stephens in Cambridge; Denis Sampson in Montreal; Ben Howard of Alfred University; Jack Morgan of the University of Missouri-Rolla; Dan Tobin and Christine Casson of Carthage College, Wisconsin; Michael Patrick Gillespie of Marquette University; and Sue Maher of the University of Nebraska-Omaha. In Dublin, I am grateful to Dermot Bolger of New Island Books, Theo Dorgan of *Poetry Ireland*, Paula Meehan, and the fabulous Philip Casey to whom this book is dedicated. Thanks are also due to Jessie Lendennie of Salmon Publishing for her encouragement and hospitality.

At Creighton University, Dean Barbara Braden of the Graduate School provided a Graduate School Summer Fellowship which allowed me to take time off from teaching and administration to work on this book. Dean Michael Proterra, S.J., of the College of Arts and Sciences awarded me travel fellowships which allowed me to present some of these chapters, in their infancies, as papers at academic conferences. I have also received tremendous support from Greg Zacharias and Mike Sundermeier, my present and former superiors in the English Department, for which I am most grateful. I also want to thank my colleagues and friends for their hospitality and their many acts of kindness extended toward me and my family since our arrival in Nebraska: Bob Churchill, Brent Spencer, Reloy Garcia, Greg Zacharias, and Annie Shahan. Also, I am very grateful to Jim, Lynn, John, and James De Mott for their friendship and support, and for keeping an eye on our home and cats when we were in Ireland.

Also, I acknowledge with gratitude a grant from the Irish Research Fund of the Irish American Cultural Institute, based in Morristown, New Jersey, which provided support for this project through the O'Shaughnessy Family, St. Paul, Minnesota.

◎

My greatest debts of gratitude are to my two families. In Ireland, I thank my parents, brothers and sisters, and their families for rich hospitality and kindness. In Omaha, Dru, Matthew, and Caitlin Wall have helped me by providing patience, tea, sympathy, and plenty of much-needed distraction which made working on this project such a fulfilling experience. If this book has a purpose, it is to record for my family in Wexford, Sligo, and Nebraska some aspects of this trip I've been on.

From the Sin-é Café to the Black Hills

One

Exile, Attitude, and the Sin-é Café
Notes on the New Irish

In his foreword to his 1993 anthology, *Ireland in Exile: Irish Writers Abroad*, which features the work of writers in their twenties and thirties, Dermot Bolger notes that the terms *"exile* and *departure* suggest an outdated degree of permanency" and that "Irish writers no longer go into exile, they simply commute" (7). Furthermore, Bolger states that a problem he encountered while editing *Ireland in Exile* "was remembering who was now back [in Ireland] and who was away" (7). Clearly, the Irish diaspora isn't what it used to be.

I belong to that generation of Irish people, born in the 1950s and 1960s, who got Irish emigration rolling again. We left Ireland en masse— our exact numbers are in dispute—and, as Dermot Bolger's anthology indicates, can be located in every pocket of the Earth. In the United States we are referred to as the New Irish. I commute between exile and Ireland, but it's an expensive business. I often wish I were another person; if that were the case, I wouldn't always have to be saving up my money to go "home," and neglecting all the other fascinating parts of the world. Commuting makes assimilation impossible.

Before coming to the United States, I worked as a teacher primarily. My purpose in coming here was to attend graduate school and experience America first-hand. This essay will provide notes on poetry, music, and the Sin-é Café in the East Village which was the center of expatriate artistic activity when I lived in New York. But I'll also look back to Ireland to see how those of my generation who have remained at home have reacted to the loss of their brothers, sisters, neighbors, and friends and I'll try to describe the "attitude" that renewed emigration has planted in the hearts and minds of my generation. An attitude is an edge to a person which indicates an undefined degree of dissatisfaction; if you know teenagers, you know what I mean. As for becoming an exile, well, that's just something I sort of fell into. I didn't actually decide in some rational manner that I was going to stay here; I just realized at some point that I was staying, since the work was here. Just like one of Dónall MacAmhlaigh's navvies, I am happy to follow the work, and am happy with my lot.

But first let's look for a minute at emigration itself and at the type of person who ended up drinking coffee or Rolling Rocks and eating pie while listening to poets read or musicians play in the Sin-é Café on St. Mark's in the East Village in the 1990s. Perhaps he or she has emerged from the following mold. In his introduction to *Ireland in Exile,* the novelist Joseph O'Connor describes candidly and bitterly the appearance in University College, Dublin, of a photographer from the Industrial Development Authority (IDA) who had been "commissioned to take pictures for an advertisement that would persuade rich foreign capitalists to open factories all over the Irish countryside" (11). The resulting photograph and its title, "The Republic of Ireland: We're the Young Europeans," is familiar to all of us who have entered Ireland in recent years. I see it in Dublin Airport at the end of the walkway when I emerge bleary-eyed from the plane.

Why does O'Connor adopt such a bitter and ironic tone? It's because most of these educated people whose faces appear in this photograph—all personally known to O'Connor—have emigrated from Ireland because they have, in common with many other college graduates, been unable to find satisfactory work or opportunities there. O'Connor believed that his future, and that of his contemporaries, was in Ireland, but this lie which had been planted in the optimistic 1960s and early 1970s was exploded by the recession which followed its blooming. O'Connor believes that the collapse of this dream of a bright future has devastated an innocent generation reared on the notion that the bad old days were over and that emigration was finished. His representation of the feelings of his generation and mine is powerful:

> You might be coming home for Christmas, or a family celebration, or a funeral, or to see a friend. Or you might just be coming back to Ireland because you're so lonely and freaked-out where you are that you can't stick it anymore, and you need a break, and you'd sell your granny to be back in the pub at home by nine o'clock on a Friday night, having fun and telling stories.
>
> And there it is, this IDA poster, illuminated at the end of the corridor that leads from the airbridge gates to the arrivals terminal: the ghostly faces of those beautiful Young Europeans. It always seems poignant as any ancient Ulster saga to me, this pantheon of departed heroes, so hopeful and innocent, frozen in their brief moment of optimism. (13)

O'Connor's words are angry but telling: By describing the unfulfilled promises a whole generation of young Irish are fleeing from and the feelings of loss and bitterness engendered by them, O'Connor is indicating just why so many of the New Irish in the United States have "attitudes." How could it be otherwise?

Joseph O'Connor is an eloquent spokesperson for his disaffected, Ryanair generation. I suppose the most notorious manifestation of this Irish "attitude" to date was Sinéad O'Connor's tearing up of the Pope's picture during her appearance on *Saturday Night Live*. In the last few years we have seen the effective dismantling of church and state in Ireland by a busy media staffed in large part by members of a lost generation, like Joseph O'Connor, who have seen family and friends gone into exile. The failures of political will and imagination in Ireland are represented subtly in Colm Tóibín's *The Heather Blazing* and with sledgehammer-like force in Dermot Bolger's harrowing and ironically titled *The Journey Home*. Irish writers of this generation, living at home and abroad, or commuting, have come to explore what Adrienne Rich has called, in a different but parallel context, "the wreck":

> I came to explore the wreck.
> The words are purposes.
> The words are maps.
> I came to see the damage that was done
> and the treasures that prevail.
> "Exploring the Wreck," 23

Although we are the commuters Dermot Bolger calls us, we still carry the same heavy emotional baggage which Irish exiles have always carried with them. Those of us—and I place myself in this group—who enjoy living in the United States are not immune from being drowned in the feelings O'Connor so eloquently describes. All of us, at home and abroad, in our edgy ways are concerned with locating internal/external "damage" and "treasures."

Although emigration is the subject of much political debate, for me it is fundamentally a personal matter. I remember one day a few years ago sitting with my father on the beach at Ardamine, County Wexford, after we had spent a long time swimming together, when he asked me if I intended to stay in America. After I answered, "Yes," he looked out silently at the sea for a long time before replying, "This wasn't supposed to happen. We worked hard and we believed that emigration was over, but here it is starting all over again. What went wrong?" There are no easy answers to this: For us Irish, emigration is both a welcome safety net and a curse. What is a fact is that everyone emerges changed from the experience, and fathers like mine who believed in the great new day of Modern Ireland have been forced to accept that things haven't worked out as planned. If some sons and daughters are confused by unfamiliar terrain, their parents are devastated by the empty bedrooms in their homes, by the silence at the dinner tables, and by the photos on the mantelpieces of the grandchildren they rarely see. By emigrating I have become a part of history and politics, which doesn't always sit well with me. Joseph O'Connor reminds me of my father to the extent that both believed in a future and were disappointed.

There's difficulty all around, but the old-fashioned wakes for those who left are a thing of the past because, as Dermot Bolger reminds us, we don't emigrate, we commute. As writers, we are not forgotten at home since Irish publishers support our efforts, and we are not unwelcome in the United States, either, as the Irish American community has shown in its efforts to win visas for us. But I believe we write our stories, poems, plays, and novels for an audience in Ireland, to remind the people that we may be gone, but are not silent. The fact that so many Irish writers live in clusters on the U.S. East Coast and in London has forced, in the words of Helena Mulkerns, "the Irish literary scene to extend its parameters to include them" (2). Added pieces to this complex puzzle have been the decisions by a variety of American writers to take up semi- or permanent residence in Ireland—Jean Valentine, Jessie Lendennie, James McCourt, Richard Tillinghast, to name just a few. Patrick Kavanagh spoke of the parochial and provincial; perhaps an appropriate binary notion for the future will be the parochial and international.

One day while waiting in the express checkout line in the Grand Union near Dyckman Street in Inwood, I started talking to the man behind me in the queue who had emigrated from Ireland forty-five years previously, and had never returned. This kind of emigrant no longer exists. Did he hate Ireland so much that he was happy to be away from it and wouldn't return under any circumstance? I remembered the relief I felt, and still do, at not having to face the prospect of permanent residence in Ireland. Similar feelings are brilliantly articulated by Rosita Boland in a poem celebrating her arrival in Australia:

> The Korean taxi-driver
> Had never heard of Ireland
> and I felt thrillingly rootless.
> "Arriving," 113

It is in part because so many of us New Irish are able to feel what Boland feels one minute and O'Connor feels the next that we have developed hard edges, or "attitudes." What has been interesting to me has been discovering similar points of view expressed in the work of such writers as Bharati Mukhergee and Sandra Cisneros about their own cultures and divided loyalties. Given that the movement of peoples from country to country is likely to increase rather than diminish in the future, it is certain that this potpourri of alienation and excitement which is reflected in contemporary writing is likely to continue to be vital in the writing of the future.

I spent many days wandering around Inwood on the way to or from the shops or park with my children in tow, and because I had children with me, people thought I was okay and would talk to me. Almost all of those elderly Irish-born people I spoke with expressed a great gratitude for the opportunity they'd received to live and work in the United States. None of them expressed such sentiments as those that appear in John Montague's poem about his mother's feelings of estrangement:

> My mother
> my mother's memories
> of America;
> a muddy cup
> she refused to drink.
> "A Muddy Cup," 66

Yet we know from the work produced by writers as various as Mary Gordon, Michael Stephens, and Pete Hamill that some wounds may have been merely covered over with Band-Aids. At the same time, it is rare to hear the New Irish declare how grateful they are for the opportunity to work in the United States: They know they have won the right to play a part in the international economy. The New Irish drink deeply of America, but retain their taut edges.

The New Irish include artists in all fields, and the work that has been produced to date, although it speaks primarily to an Irish-based audience, should be accessible to all Americans since no aspect of contemporary American life is immune to the effects of migration: region to region, state to state, city to city, suburb to suburb, and so on. These recent exiles have not bought into the ancient culture of emigration, but have fallen backward into it, updating and transforming it in the process. But here a distinction should be considered if not insisted on. When I think of these artists, I am concerned with people who did not arrive in the United States with artistic identities in place, but who came here to begin, or continue, the process of gaining or developing identities as poets, novelists, musicians, or painters. Some Irish writers who arrived before the current wave have ignored the immigrant experience altogether—they have neither felt it nor been moved by living in the United States, and it has had little or no effect on their themes or forms, whereas other writers have been absolutely energized by their experience of America—Brian Moore, Eavan Boland, James Liddy, Eamon Grennan. But the raw New Irish are very much engaged with American culture and none are afraid of it, having spent their childhoods in the 1960s and 1970s growing up on it. They haven't come to the United States to reap the rewards for their artistic endeavors, but to learn the artists' ropes on American, not native, soil.

What one finds in the poetry written by commuters is a mixture of alienation and excitement. These exiles of Erin may be better educated and use more sophisticated forms and language than their predecessors from earlier generations who created melodies and lyrics, but they frequently share common sentiments and a sense of loss. The young Irish certainly know that when they leave school or college they will enter a global economy and will be as likely—in fact, much more likely—to find work in Frankfurt, Chicago, or London as in Dublin or Cork; however, even though each and every one of them knows this, and understands that emigration is a way of life for Irish people, they are often still overwhelmed by feelings of loss when they settle away from Ireland. And the poetry and music produced by the voices of this new generation, my own included, frequently express such feelings. Take for example these lines from a Sara Berkeley poem describing California:

> I was not built for
> the dull rumble of the valley air,
> the great steel birds
> that fly with a dark grey
> whine, grazing the sky.
>
> "Fault," 76

Take away the twentieth-century *topoi,* and Berkeley's poem of displacement could just as easily be referring to those exiles who had arrived in France and Spain in the wake of the Nine Years' War. A similar line of thinking can be found in many of Greg Delanty's poems written since coming to the United States:

> Perhaps now I understand the meaning of home
> for I'm in a place, but it is not in me
>
> "Home from Home," 16

The final lines of this same poem suggest that the New Irish, instead of being able to trade the unemployment and unhappiness of home for the wealth and freedoms of the New World, have fallen into the ancient core of exile and are repeating the lives lived out by their predecessors. Frequently in his work, the theme is exile, the tone sorrowful:

> I'll introduce you to all & sundry,
> even to those who are dead & gone,
> or just gone, unable to make home at home.
> When time is called we'll stagger from this poem.
>   "Home from Home," 16

What is interesting, though, is that when Delanty celebrates American life, as he does in the final poems of *Southward*, he abandons the closed and traditional forms which characterize his poems set in Ireland—and the poems which describe his feelings of separation and alienation from home—and adopts open or Whitmanesque American poetic forms to celebrate America:

> Beneath the green fountain
> of a palm tree
> a duck loiters on one leg
> with wings in white pockets . . .
> I blaze, blessed
> by the brilliance of them all.
>   "Observations," 45

To be able to write convincingly about America, the contemporary Irish poet must be able to partly unlearn what he or she has picked up in Ireland and produce newer hybrid forms which are part-Irish and part-American. For the New Irish who have sought their artistic voices in the United States, their facility at being able to absorb American influences and styles has been crucial to their success, as is evidenced by the work of writers as diverse as Delanty, Berkeley, Nuala Archer, Emer Martin, Gerard Donovan, Helena Mulkerns, and Colum McCann. Perhaps the perfectly formed artistic work combines the precise closed forms employed by many Irish poets with the open forms of American poets: Perfection lies somewhere between Derek Mahon and Anne Waldman. That old themes such as exile and loss are being recorded using new, open forms represents an important development in Irish writing. A generation of exiles/expatriates/commuters is writing its own story as it goes along—a tapestry is being created minute by minute.

The meeting and performance place for many of the New York–based Irish exiles was the Sin-é Café in the East Village. It was such a remarkable financial and cultural success that it became a kind of icon of an age and was even written up in the *New Yorker*'s "Rock and Folk" section, which suggests the extent to which those who had been a part of that scene had made waves in the cultural marketplace. Previously, Irish expatriate artists involved themselves in American artistic and cultural movements and undergrounds; what happened at the Sin-é was that the sassy New Irish created their own cultural movement, one which was part-Irish, part-East Village, and which was unashamedly ethnic and multicultural. The Sin-é had more in common with the Nuyorican Café than it did with the uptown Irish American Historical Society. Of course, it was founded as a café, not as a cultural society; however, it drew in artists and provided them with stages on which to perform. The Sin-é was a postmodern, downtown, fin de siècle Gaelic Park with attitude.

If you had heard all the good words about the Sin-é and you went there with your head full of wonders, your heart would have dropped when you walked in the door, but, as the *New Yorker* noted:

> Don't be misled by the sleepy, hole-in-the wall atmosphere of this bohe-
> mian Irish café, or by the fact that the place has no stage. While patrons
> have been writing in their journals, rolling cigarettes, or lingering over
> their Rolling Rocks, some pretty fine musicians have turned up and tuned
> up: Sinead O'Connor, Marianne Faithfull, and Luka Bloom. (18)

The relaxed ambience of the Sin-é was in keeping with the anti-establishment mood of Shane Doyle, its creator, and his patrons. The readings and sessions, often put together by the writer/journalist/United Nations translator Helena Mulkerns, reflected this predominant zeitgeist. In my last years in New York, I attended some remarkable readings and heard some great music there: readings by poets Nuala Ní Dhomhnaill and Rita Ann Higgins and novelist Colm Tóibín. You never knew who'd drop in. One afternoon while I was sipping a coffee, I looked up and saw Mike Scott of the Waterboys (one of my all-time heroes) sitting across the room. I pointed him out to my kids, who were hard at work on their sodas, but they didn't believe that he was *really* the man who sang "Fisherman's Blues." They reckoned I was joking. Helena Mulkerns's most elaborate organizational feat was her "Bloomsday in the East Village" on June 16, 1991. This cabaret reading/performance of *Ulysses* had a cast of forty or fifty people—it was often difficult to tell who was in the cast and who was in the audience—and went on riotously for twelve hours. The odyssey began in the Sin-é before proceeding to other East Village hostelries. People are still talking about it, but not about my off-off-off Broadway debut as an "actor" in that extravaganza.

I was enormously grateful that the Sin-é was there when I lived in New York. It was exciting to come downtown on the A train from Inwood and walk across St. Mark's to listen, read, and drink, to be involved in a great adventure. The Sin-é was a vibrant emotional and artistic home-away-from-home, which bridged the divide between two countries and which provided writers, painters, and musicians with a meeting place. Such venues are vital because they act as magnets for developing artists and give them the stepping stones, exposure, and confidence they need. It was great that it existed while I was there; great that it was Irish; great that it was so casual; and great (and significant socially and historically) that Irish people could move at such ease, be right at home in the East Village. The New Irish looked like everyone else downtown—well, maybe not everybody, but you know what I mean. The distance in cultural terms between St. Mark's and Temple Bar in Dublin has grown so small that it's no longer worth calculating. Eventually, the Sin-é was sold, then renovated, then closed, now passed into folklore. But now there are other cafés—Anseo and the Scratcher are two—in the neighborhood which have grown up under the Sin-é's influence and which provide a similar kind of ambience. Also of note was the appearance in 1994 and 1995 of the first three issues of *Here's Me Bus,* edited by Martin Mahoney and Colin Lacey, which is full of the words and art of the New Irish and heavy with attitude.

The healthy clash between present and past and the subsequent merging of forms and genres is exuberantly manifested in the CDs and live performances of Black 47. I heard them first in the Sin-é and later in Paddy Reilly's at Twenty-eighth Street and Second Avenue. Into their traditional Irish core are mixed layers of reggae, rap, hip-hop, and new wave, and the result is a dynamic hybrid—a music simultaneously Irish and urban American. Larry Kirwan, Black 47's principal writer, is much more tuned in to the America of the margins than he is to the central cultural matrix: Because the center didn't hold at home, because exiles feel marginalized, they are inclined to gravitate toward the comfort of the margins in search of those who share their concerns. But there is always the sense in America that the margins possess the energy for change and are rising with the tide. Kirwan is not alone in this among Irish artists: U2's *Rattle and Hum* and Roddy Doyle's *The Commitments* are homages to African American music and culture; Paul Muldoon has gravitated toward Native America; and Eavan Boland has found kindred spirits among American feminists. Intense contact with America has had a huge influence on what and how these people have written: The contact has empowered them. But they have gone to the margins, away from the center and from traditional Irish America. Immigrants, in a political climate in which the political right and some elements of the center and left seek to marginalize and expel them, will continue to gravitate toward the invisibility and warmth of the urban margins.

Larry Kirwan's songs describe and celebrate the lives of the New Irish in New York, and they, like their subjects, are full of hope, failure, and ambivalence. His typical protagonist seeks self-definition, and this is done by poking fun at those who lack style, at least as he defines it:

> We got a gig in the Village Pub
> but the regulars there all said that we sucked.
> Then Big John Flynn, said "Oh, no no,
> you'll be causin' a riot if I don't let you go."
>
> Then a flintstone from the Phoenix gave us a call,
> but when he heard the beat, he was quite appalled.
> "D'yez not know nothin' by Christy Morre?"
> The next thing you'll be wantin' is Danny Boy!
>
> "Rockin' the Bronx"

And Kirwan's Irish exile is one of the commuters Dermot Bolger describes; however, the commuter is caught in the situation of being able to visit Ireland, but not stay:

> Sit down by the fire, put your feet on the grate
> spend the night reminiscin' 'til the hour grows late.
> Always remember at the end of the day
> you can always go home, you just can't stay.
>
> "American Wake"

Of course, it is by no means certain that the returned exile wants to remain at home for longer than a couple of weeks.

On the back cover of *Ireland in Exile* is a photograph which defines the attitude I have been discussing: a young man with an odd fade-like haircut has his back to the camera. One hand is placed behind his back and he is giving the viewer "the finger." Against whom is this directed? It's directed at everybody and nobody, at Ireland, the United States, and the rest of the world. It's full of significance, and it's infantile. It's a gesture of the dispossessed, and a gesture of the new arrival in the United States as he or she heads for the margin. The New Irish seek to bite the hands of history which both deny and feed.

After a lull, Irish immigration to the United States resumed. Between the 1980s and early 1990s, a wave of New Irish arrived in America and set up camp, and began the process of defining in their own words what it means to be Irish women and men who live in America at the end of the twentieth century. Now, the Celtic Tiger roars loudly from Ireland a mighty song of prosperity and employment. For the present, the ranks of the New Irish will no longer swell, but you never know what's going to happen to the Irish economy. What we all have learned is that the good times don't last forever.

Two

The Long Journey Home to Brooklyn
Michael Stephens's Books of the Dead

The good reviews which Michael Stephens has received for his most recent novel, *The Brooklyn Book of the Dead* (1994), coupled with his being awarded a major prize for his selected essays, *Green Dreams: Essays under the Influence of the Irish* (1994), have meant that the work of a talented, but neglected, Irish American writer has at last begun to find a wider audience. His major theme is migration, and in his hands this is a complex and fascinating concept which involves not only the movement of Irish Americans from Brooklyn to Long Island, but also Stephens's own journey as an artist. His *Season at Coole* and *The Brooklyn Book of the Dead* are works which can indeed be understood in relation to the Irish American tradition, but they will also force us to look outside of that tradition if we wish to appreciate them fully. In addition, to find Stephens's literary partners it is necessary to look beyond the worlds of Mary Gordon and John Gregory Dunne, among whom Stephens does not belong, and examine instead the work of the African American writer Trey Ellis, the Latina writer Sandra Cisneros, and the Scottish writer James Kelman. It is ironic that at a time when the Irish are seen to have become completely assimilated into mainstream America, one of the group's most important literary voices can be best read as a "minority" writer. Is it possible that the Irish have not been as completely assimilated as some would like us to believe?

The world which we are presented with in the two Coole family novels is brilliantly created but full of gritty reality and dark humor which allows the reader to experience fully what Thomas McGonigle has called "the taste of sour ash" (174). The movement of the Cooles from East New York to Mineola and the negative effect that it has had on the family certainly confirms Lawrence J. McCaffrey's notion that the movement of Irish Americans from ghetto to suburbs after World War II often represented a sad progress "from someplace to no place" (*The Irish Diaspora in America*, 152–78). A high-tempered family such as the Cooles requires a high-energy environment to sustain them, but the remote suburbs cannot answer this need:

> These folks were from the slums, the Coole tribe, but they didn't have their ghetto no more, they had to make a private shitheap within the heart of a suburban area, working as antibodies to the cancer around them, though the community thought them the malignancy, the old man got a new citation from the town government once a month, rundown house, improper shingles on roof, broken windows, garage in condemnable shape, hedges too high, litter obstructing pedestrian traffic that passed his door, they needed a subway the Cooles, a place to hang out, scribbling their graffiti on the walls, instead they did it on the walls of their castle, their Alamo. (*Season at Coole*, 161–62)

In contrast, East New York in particular and Brooklyn in general, referred to as "Mecca" and "Jerusalem," are alive and "gleaming, sweating with humidity and heat, bursting with an aroma that promised to go sour in a day or two" (*The Brooklyn Book of the Dead*, 136–37). The city, because it forces people to live close to one another, is vital and lively and awakens the senses, but suburbia forces the Cooles to turn in on themselves and consume one another using hatred, anger, poverty, drugs, and alcohol as their weapons. But when Leland Coole dies his wake is held in Brooklyn because Brooklyn is "that ancient ground" (*BBD*, 17) and "it would be East New York or nothing" (*BBD*, 15).

The old neighborhood, however, symptomatic of the decline which is evident in many parts of urban America, has become hostile—two of the Cooles are mugged outside the funeral parlor—and it is impossible for the children to fulfill the stipulations contained in their father's will:

> Another one of his demands was that the funeral parlor where he would be laid out had to be the one across from Our Lady of Lourdes, and afterward they would wake him in the bars along Broadway underneath the elevated subway train—how was he to know that all the bars would be boarded up and replaced by crack houses and bootleggers and numbers parlors? (*BBD*, 14)

The Cooles have fared no better than the old neighborhood: Emmet Coole is an alcoholic cab driver "determined to become the oldest crackhead in history"; Terry is a derelict who lives in an abandoned school bus on Long Island; a number of them have been in trouble with the law for a variety of petty crimes; and one son is in the Witness Protection Program (*BBD*, 62). Except for Jackie, the eldest, who takes lithium, they all appear to be heavy drinkers and drug abusers.

It would certainly be an understatement to say, despite the wonderful grotesque humor which is present, that these novels present an unhappy view of Irish America. Clearly, Stephens writes out of anger and is ambivalent toward his background. Novels like *The Brooklyn Book of the Dead* do not always find favor with arbiters of Irish American taste who object to such bleak views of the Irish American world being presented without the benefits of softening contexts. Reviewing a recent anthology of Irish American writing in *Éire-Ireland,* Ron Ebest wonders "why, among the work of nearly sixty contributors to the anthology, the only aspect of Irishness that is thoroughly explored is its gruesomeness. The effect of reading this dreary anthology . . . is like standing on a streetcorner in an alien city, and watching the passage of a parade of grotesques" (182). It is true that Irish American writers usually present their ethnic group in an unflattering light; in this regard Stephens and Mary Gordon have much in common. However, this modus operandi, which has long been a feature of Irish and Irish American writing, is part of the writer's historical inheritance. Did Joyce present Dublin in a flattering light? Should we dismiss Brian Moore's *The Lonely Passion of Judith Hearne,* Edna O'Brien's *The Country Girls Trilogy,* and Dermot Bolger's *The Journey Home* because they present a gruesome view of Ireland? To be sure, Irish writers, in both America and Ireland, exhibit an almost pathological attraction to life's down side, but the work remains strong, if harsh and without comfort.

Ebest implies that Irish American writers are guilty of stereotyping, and certainly this is present in Stephens's Coole novels. Of stereotyping Stephens has argued:

> You think about stereotypes, but the thing is that sometimes truths can be revealed through them. In the end I guess you just have to write what you know. The strange thing is that you can take these people and put them in Brooklyn or Long Island and they just don't change that much. They might as well be back in Dublin. (*Irish Echo,* 41)

In the world that Stephens creates the suburb and the changed ghetto become metaphors for alienation and assimilation, and represent locations where the American dream is dismantled. But should we look on the Cooles as typical or see them as exceptions to the norm? Lawrence J. McCaffrey believes that "with some individual and geographic exceptions, the American Irish have been assimilated and have earned a comfortable standard of living and respectability in the United States as relatively contented citizens" (*Textures of Irish America,* xi). But Kerby Miller disagrees, believing that McCaffrey and others place "an ahistorical overemphasis on the ultimate suburbanization and embourgeoisement of the Irish that trivializes the immigrant and even the second generation experiences" (*American Historical Review,* 1394). In the first- and second-generation Irish Americans in Stephens's work one finds much of what Miller defines as "the pain of exile; poverty, exploitation, and conflict (both inter- and intraethnic); the strains and disappointments of assimilation; and what [James T.] Farrell called the 'tragedy of the worker'" (*AHR,* 1394). John Gregory Dunne contends that Irish Americans proceed from "immigrant" to "outcast" to "assimilated" to "deracinated" and both Greeley and McCaffrey appear to agree with this thesis (*Textures of Irish America,* 176). However, the Cooles have not assimilated. Perhaps they are an exception when considered in relation to the majority of Irish Americans, but they are hardly exceptional when considered in relation to Americans as a whole. The Cooles are shadow Americans to whom Stephens gives voice and who reclaim for themselves minority status. Arthur Schlesinger, Jr., has produced the following axiom to explain the process of assimilation: "Not only must *they* want assimilation and integration; *we* must want assimilation and integration too" (*The Disuniting of America,* 19). The Cooles did want to achieve both, but it did not work out and they have become one of many families who have fallen overboard from the boat of the American Dream. They do not, to turn Thomas Paine's words on their head, "have it in [their] power to begin the world all over again" (quoted in *The Disuniting of America,* 23). Such Irish Americans are hardly alone in contemporary America.

Michael Stephens and Kerby Miller present rather bleak views of the progress of Irish Americans especially when contrasted with the optimism one finds in the writings of Andrew Greeley and Lawrence J. McCaffrey. McCaffrey believes that Miller is of a generation that became embittered and detached from America as a result of the "American involvement in Vietnam and the presidencies of Lyndon Johnson and Richard Nixon," and "in describing Irish-American alienation in the past, they are expressing more of their own present day ambivalences about their country than the sentiments of the Irish in the United States" (*Textures of Irish America,* xiii). Miller, on the other hand, believes that studies like McCaffrey's *The Irish in Chicago* "in some respects mark a regression to a celebratory 'contributions to the making of America' style that has plagued ethnic history since its inception" (*AHR,*1394). Clearly, the dispute is a generational one divided by the Kennedy Era—the one concerned with rising and joy, the other with falling and rage. This conflict is well dramatized in the falling-out which took place in 1969 between Alfred Kazin and his son Michael. The younger Kazin remembers that his father "didn't want to take the point of view that America was an evil place" (Smith, 3). But Michael Stephens *is* an "Irish American writer—I think of myself both as a Brooklyn writer and an Irish-American writer," and he is ambivalent; however, ambivalence is very much a part of the literary baggage carried around by the postmodern, post-Camelot, American writer (*Irish Echo,* 41).

Although *Season at Coole* and *The Brooklyn Book of the Dead* are firmly rooted in contemporary America, they belong very much within the Irish American tradition. In particular, one can argue that Stephens's novels are postmodern versions of James T. Farrell's *Studs Lonigan.* Writing of *Studs Longian,* Charles Fanning discovers three important central concerns in Farrell's novel: "the goal of home ownership; the matriarch as moral exemplar; and the Christian ideal of the happy death" (*Studs Lonigan,* xxiii). The goal of home ownership is explored in *Season at Coole* by the movement of the Cooles from Brooklyn to Long Island, which parallels a similar move by the Lonigans from their building on Michigan Avenue to South Shore. And, as Fanning explains, the Lonigan family's move to the newer, all-white neighborhood of South Shore "also contributes to Studs's failure to find his way in the world. Denied the sustaining context of home in a familiar neighborhood, Studs becomes even more of an aimless drifter" (*Studs Lonigan,* xxiv). These comments are equally applicable to all of the Coole family. Mrs. Coole is a moral exemplar until, worn down by abuse, overwork, and childbearing, she becomes an alcoholic and eventual parody of a moral exemplar:

> Mother Rose plopped on the laundry she was to wash, already high and wanting to get higher, she opened the vodka bottle first, drank a good swill and washed that down with a nip from the muscatel bottle, she was talking out loud, but not loud enough for her son, the other side of the cellar partition, to hear. Her dress was akimbo past her thighs, the buttons opened at the top, her hair kinky and uncombed, her smell pungently alcoholic and lonely, whimpering, whispering, holding court with the Virgin Mary, who she often saw and spoke with, while drunk in her part of the cellar. (*Season at Coole,* 15)

In *The Brooklyn Book of the Dead,* the happy death is both explored and mocked, the former by the bringing of Inspector Coole's body back to Brooklyn, the latter by the high jinks that take place in and around the funeral home.

Fanning has argued of William Kennedy that Kennedy emerged from "a solid literary context" and that the presence of such writers as Farrell and Edwin O'Connor made it possible for Kennedy "to strike out on his own" and to "explore the harsh reality of Irish-America" (*The Irish Voice in America,* 351). Michael Stephens is following in this tradition and taking Irish American fiction another mile in distance and depth. He is involved in a process which Harold Bloom, writing of poetry, has called *tessera,* which casts light on Stephens's relationship to James T. Farrell:

> A Poet antithetically "completes" his precursor, by so reading the parent-poem as to retain its terms but to mean them in another sense, as though the precursor had failed to go far enough. (*The Anxiety of Influence,* 14)

In respect of influence and anxiety, it is interesting to note that in the essays on writers which appear in *Green Dreams,* none deal with Irish American or even American writers—all of Stephens's literary heroes are Europeans and most of these Europeans are Irish.

Language is the writer's tool, and when Stephens needed a language to accommodate his own literary vision he found it in Joyce:

> Even today, knowing better, one can still abide by some of the childhood legends about James Joyce, that one's infatuations with him are not completely literary. Even being American, and raised more in the ways of American culture, the residues of that Irish past seem to imbue one's life and writings, and there is still an attitude, cultivated, no doubt, from those early myths of James Joyce, that suggests that English is a foreign language, and that coming from an Irish background one has an obligation to use this language in two ways. The first is to write it better than any native speaker . . . and second, to subvert that language at every chance, knowing that the tradition you have inherited is one of experimentation. The tradition is to be original, un-English, and never bend in the pursuit of those ideals, no matter how impossible they may seem, and probably are. I blame James Joyce for instilling these attitudes in us. (*Green Dreams,* 77–78)

Stephens's concerns about language echo those which have been articulated by many writers in Ireland. The poet John Montague, taking stock of the fact that history has deprived the Irish of their language, refers to English, which he employs in his work, as "a grafted tongue" through which experience and feeling emerge uncomfortably:

> . . . To grow
> a second tongue, as
> harsh a humiliation
> as twice to be born.
> "A Grafted Tongue," 37

In *Station Island,* Seamus Heaney calls forth the spirit of Joyce, who reminds him that now "the English language belongs to us" (93). Irish writers have grafted English to their mother tongue and produced a hybrid language and a subversive literature. Hiberno-English, the English language as it is spoken in Ireland, is related to Stephens's "un-English"

(*Green Dreams,* 78). From Joyce, Stephens has journeyed to Brian O'No-lan, whose *An Béal Bocht* is an important influence on the Coole novels, to Yeats, Beckett, and James Stephens. It is abundantly clear from the essays that Michael Stephens looks toward Ireland for confirmation and away from Irish America; however, like the Liffey in *Finnegans Wake,* he ends up at the source (like Leland Coole for his wake) in Brooklyn. Also, Stephens's thoughts on language are similar to those articulated by Stephen Dedalus in the well-known funnel/tundish debate with the English dean in *A Portrait of the Artist as a Young Man* in which the young student shows the dean how the English language has undergone a transformation in Ireland. To be able to write of a hard and cruel world, the writer must create a hard and cruel language: He must make the oppressor's language his own. Michael Stephens, to write of Irish Americans who have fallen off the gravy train, has invented such a language—one which brings these people painfully and brilliantly to life.

"The use of history as therapy means the corruption of history as history," Arthur Schlesinger, Jr., has written (93). We might as easily apply the same axiom to literature. Certainly, Stephens's fiction is neither therapeutic nor comforting, and his esthetic is similar to that of Reginald Hudlin, an African American filmmaker, who is against black films "which [are] more obsessed with being good PR for the race than with being culturally authentic" (quoted in Ellis, 239). The philosopher Arthur Danto has called the work by the new African American artists "disturbatory art—art that shakes you up" (quoted in Ellis, 239). This is put even more colorfully by Vernon Reid of the rock band Living Colour: "When you look into your own shit and dig in, then you'll find the universal. You won't find the universal by deciding to go after the universal" (quoted in Ellis, 242). By examining the Cooles in detail, Stephens reveals truths about contemporary America. What Trey Ellis calls the "New Black Aesthetic" is remarkably close to Michael Stephens's esthetic. It is remarkable that many of the artists whom Ellis labels as being part of the "New Black Aesthetic" (and this group includes the rappers Public Enemy) are, like Stephens, the products of Long Island upbringings.

And the Latina writer Sandra Cisneros has had to wrestle with language and identity in ways that Stephens and Ellis have, as she makes clear in the short story "*Bien* Pretty":

> ¡*Ay!* To make love in Spanish, in a manner as intricate and devout as La Alhambra. To have a lover sigh *mi vida, mi preciosa, mi chiquitita,* and whisper things in that language crooned to babies, that language mur-

mured by grandmothers, those words that smelled like your house, like flour tortillas, and the inside of your daddy's hat, like everyone talking in the kitchen at the same time, or sleeping with the windows open, like sneaking cashews from the crumpled quarter-pound bag Mama always hid in her lingerie drawer after she went shopping with Daddy at the Sears. (*Woman Hollering Creek,* 153)

If the writer exists outside of the national literary discourse, he or she must create what Stephens calls an "un-English" (*Green Dreams,* 78) so that the product will, at least in Cisneros's case, smell "like your house [and] like flour tortillas" (*Woman Hollering Creek,* 153). Cisneros, like James T. Farrell, is from Chicago, and her novel *The House on Mango Street,* like *Studs Lonigan,* is concerned with immigrant life there. Of course, it would be foolish to generalize too much; nevertheless, it is clear that Irish American writers share with their African American and Latin contemporaries an active interest in the connection between language and identity.

Another writer we can profitably compare with Stephens is the Scottish writer James Kelman. When Kelman was awarded the Booker Prize in 1994 for *How Late It Was, How Late,* a storm broke out. Simon Jenkins of the *London Times* called the novel "literary vandalism . . . and the ramblings of a Glaswegian drunk" (October 28, 1994). Kelman, on the other hand, at the award ceremony "made a rousing case for the culture and language of 'indigenous' people outside of London" (Lyall, *New York Times*). It should be noted that the winner of the Booker Prize the previous year was Roddy Doyle for *Paddy Clarke Ha Ha Ha,* another writer who has found a new language for the shadow Northside Dubliners of Barrytown. Doyle is connected to America through his interest in its blues, soul, and rock music (he took the name Barrytown from a Steely Dan song), whereas Stephens is connected to Ireland through its literature. Of course, popular music is one of America's many great exports, whereas literature is one of Ireland's few. It is never difficult for the Irish American writer to become involved in cultural exchanges with Ireland or vice-versa: In each case, because the two countries are so closely bound by immigration/emigration and a shared history, the writer is embarking on a journey home.

To conclude, *Season at Coole* and *The Brooklyn Book of the Dead* are proof of the continuing vitality of the Irish American tradition in fiction. These are tough books designed not to make the reader comfortable (but what great writing ever does this?) but to brilliantly bring to life the world of those shadow Irish Americans whose province is the edge of America, who are fading and dying. These are works by a brilliant novelist-critic that connect Irish American writing to the writing of shadow people everywhere, that force us to rethink our conceptions of Irish America and to assert perhaps that the old ancestral links between Ireland and Irish America are more alive than we think.

Three

Immigration, Technology, and Sense of Place

Those days when I wasn't working I enjoyed going 'round the corner to Chris and Louis Discount (they were immigrants from Greece), buying a newspaper, a cup of coffee ("Best coffee in New York," Louis said), and some sweets for the kids and then heading up Broadway, pushing the stroller in the direction of Inwood Park. I was Louis's sometime secretary: If he was having difficulty communicating with the *Times*, the *News*, or the *Post*, he'd ask me to phone on his behalf. He thought that I spoke the same kind of English the people in the billing sections of the city's newspapers did. I shouted at the people on the other end of the line to get their respect. Shouting became my standard telephone technique; it was the only method that worked for me in New York.

Louis's hands were black from handling the papers and I remember him bent over the sports pages of the Greek newspaper reading the reports of soccer games from Europe. We shared a common language—Gullit, Shearer, Platini, Barcelona, Maradona—which brought us close, separating me from the Americans, or Yankees as he called them with a smile, who came into his shop. This is why some mornings Louis would place a stack of bills on the counter, hand me the phone, and say the coffee's free today. Of course, the Dominicans spoke this language too, but they had their own newspaper shops, their own loyalties. It was to their bodegas I went in the evenings for bottles of beer and quarts of milk. There, men stood talking in groups and parted to let me through. The Dominicans knew, too, that Jack Charlton managed the Irish soccer team.

One morning, in typical New York fashion, the shop was closed, Louis was gone, and the rumor went around that he was working in a restaurant in Connecticut. So I transferred my business, for what it was worth, to a shop on Broadway owned by a man from Galicia in Spain—"We are both Celts," he said to me when he got to know me better. Later, when I told him I was leaving New York to live in Nebraska he shook his head and

moaned, "You are leaving New York to live in America. God help you!!"
I still can see Pedro leaning across the counter to make a point; he is
always smiling.

I often think of Louis in Connecticut working in a diner, if they have
diners in Connecticut. He must be the counterman pouring coffee, yelling
orders taken over the phone at the chef, smiling as he hands you back
your change. Maybe he's telling the customers that he's happy to be out
of the crazy city, or maybe he remembers New York fondly. I know he
misses Greece and is saving money to go home: the old story. I think too
of the immigrant businesses which define New York for me—newspaper
shops and kiosks underground, bakeries, diners, delis, and fruit vendors.
I think too that each moment in the city men and women are reading,
or looking forward to reading, newspapers which tell the news of their
homelands, and I see myself leaning over their shoulders, sharing in their
excitement and anticipation, like a child who, unable to read, studies the
pictures carefully and invents the narrative.

Up Broadway we went—past the shops and the old Dyckman House.
At 207th Street (to the right) stood the Tara Gift Shop where each Monday night a crowd of Irish people waited to buy Irish newspapers hot off
the plane. Piles of local papers, just like at Eason's bookshop in Dublin,
and Irish hands and Irish eyes eager for the news of home. After a couple
of years, I gave up buying these papers: It was unsettling to get this news
so fast, to seem to be living in Ireland, but to be so distant from it. The
Echo and the *Voice*, both published in New York, provide the sports re-
sults, my dad the local news, and that's all I need. Which coalition is in
power or what Fianna Fáil is up to doesn't bother me; I don't care about
that stuff.

Now, ironically, a few years on, living in Nebraska and far away from
an Irish center of influence in America, it's become even easier for me to
get the news from Ireland. And it's free. Each morning at work, I turn on
my computer and read the *Irish Times*. Everything is there at my finger-
tips. I can even convince my superiors that this reading is related to my
writing and research. It is quite a measure of success for me as an employee to be able to tell my employer that spending the first half-hour of
company time reading a newspaper is vital to my work. Even more of a
triumph is to know that my superiors will believe me, encourage me, and
suggest that soon I'll need to be provided with a better machine so that
the graphics will come up clearer and the text will appear with greater
speed. I know I have made it in America! The first section I read is the
sports; then, I work my way backward through the other sections. This is
the way I have always read newspapers, my tao of reading. It seemed so

natural to me as a child that the first page of the *Irish Times* contained the national and international news and the second the daily racing runners and riders. How could it ever be possible to justify another set of priorities?

Yet despite the convenience and addictiveness of the Internet, a part of me regrets its power, presence, and intrusiveness. Certainly, it is exciting to get Irish news so easily, to have at least a sense that I know what is happening in Ireland. In the old days, you had to be an embassy employee to get news that fast. It fascinated me as a student in Dublin to look at the antennas on top of Iveagh House and to think of all the secret communiques which the Department of Foreign Affairs were sending out to their ambassadors and consuls throughout the world. With hindsight I suspect that the diplomatic staff awaited the same news I hungered for—scores from championship matches and county finals.

But the immigrant needs also to be able to forget, to be able to walk away down some distant road, to look ahead and see bright neon signs and people on benches in the sun who are curious about him or her. Turning to look behind, the immigrant should find revealed a clear, open sky. Of course, we cannot forget. I will always walk from my parents' house to school: each morning noting the presence of the train, the presence of the river, the time on the clock above Kerr's shop, these minutes before nine o'clock when the life of the town seemed mute and suspended. The Internet provides us with information, but it doesn't allow us the illusion of forgetting and fails to nourish us. We are reminded that we are not over there, which makes adjustment to America more difficult. To survive, we need to be able to begin the process of forgetting. Paradoxically, being Irish, our deepest desire is to remember and re-create everything.

On these weekday mornings the streets were alive and sparkling, and I felt very strongly the romance of living in New York. When we sat on a bench outside the Dyckman House I'd watch what my kids were watching, knowing what they were learning was not what I had learned on the Square or on the prom in Enniscorthy in the 1960s. Because it was so different, it seemed richer. And just as the street sweeper (the cleaner, not the gun) transfixed my children so too I was transfixed by their intense watching. And we observed the man on the next bench who fed corn to the squirrels, who called them out from the trees by the names he'd christened them—Jenny, Terry, and Sara. The buses and gypsy caps paraded up and down Broadway all day long, and I was a child again among children, feeling intensely privileged, beginning (I was thinking) to finally understand America. Occasionally, theater stopped the world: a fire department truck and hook-and-ladder convoy was called out to a false alarm on 215th Street.

When we got to the playground, the children ran to the equipment and sandbox while I sat down to drink my coffee and read my paper. It was great not to have to work every weekday. At that time I was working part-time in the Bronx at Hostos Community College on 149th and Grand Concourse where it seemed every student was from another country. One day I asked the students what the "Gettysburg Address" was all about, but they had never heard of it, and this made me feel right at home since there have been so many ordinary things about America which I have had to learn too. One day not long after I arrived, a woman I was chatting up asked me if I liked Pop Tarts, and she couldn't understand why I hadn't heard of them and thought I was some sort of freak. I'm not a freak; I'm an alien. My wife has taken on the job of explaining America to me, of cutting through this confusion. It was she who put together my packet for immigration after I had failed at the task myself and was pushed away from the grill in Federal Plaza. At night, before falling asleep beside her, the blinds closed, the air conditioner humming dreamily, I feel so firmly rooted here.

The teaching work was okay because it brought me into new neighborhoods and introduced me to new people. Some mornings on the way to the Bronx, while waiting for the bus at 145th and Broadway in Harlem, I'd hear (when I closed my eyes) the jazz of older times, the voice of Billie Holiday, and smell the sweet aroma of perfume from an elegant lady stepping from a huge, late model Eldorado. Then, to match my mood, I'd recite to myself some lines by Langston Hughes:

> Have you dug the spill
> Of Sugar Hill?
> Cast your gims
> On this sepia thrill:
> Brown sugar lassie,
> Caramel treat,
> Honey-gold baby
> Sweet enough to eat.
> Peach-skinned girlie,
> Coffee and cream,
> Chocolate darling
> Out of a dream.
> "Harlem Sweeties," 245

Between 7 and 7:30 A.M. the streets were quiet. I waited with a bunch of kids in uniforms headed for Cardinal Hayes High School across the river, and we all got into the bus via the rear door. One day I remember our bus passing Mitch "Blood" Green, who'd fought Mike Tyson in the ring and on the street, and the kids waved and hollered at him. Another day, an old hand in the department I worked in answered my comment that the boss seemed a decent sort of guy with the comment that "he should be institutionalized." A year later, I sat in the office of the English Department awaiting news of my teaching load and responsibilities for the semester, with my contract in my bag. It seemed I sat for hours until I was told there was no work. This is how my career in the Bronx ended.

While the children made friends with one another, I made friends with the mothers and fathers. Every stereotype and cliche that I'd ever heard about the city and its people was exploded by these encounters in the playground. New Yorkers, I discovered, are a gentle, friendly, and communal people, despite all the negative hype. Because we lived so intensely and close to each other in such a crowded city, we were forced by circumstances to get on with each other, to be neighborly, to be friendly, to talk to each other on the stairways of our apartment buildings, to sit together on the benches in the park watching our children play. One day a bookish-looking mother sat beside me and produced a sheet of paper from her tote bag and placed it in my hands. "I've been reading *The Commitments*," said she, "and don't know what these words mean, and since you're from Ireland. . . ." I looked at the sheet and laughed. It read "bollix" and "gobshite." Bollix I dispatched in my best Bakhtinian metaphor/metonomy fashion, but gobshite was more difficult. I told the lady that if you didn't recognize a gobshite when you saw one, you had a problem. I understood that just as there were things about America I would never understand, there were also things about Ireland I could never satisfactorily explain to someone who'd never lived that singular, Irish life.

When my son Matthew started school he went to P.S. 98: He was in a bilingual English/Spanish program. His teacher said he had a real flair for Spanish and one day asked me whether I spoke Spanish and helped him. I (proudly) declared to her: "Well, I've picked up a lot of Spanish since coming to Inwood. I listen to the super of my building speak Spanish, I listen to the men in the bodega and the diner. . . ." She stopped me dead in my tracks and said, pointing a finger at me, "Under no condition speak Spanish to your son," and she pulled him toward her to protect him from his Spanglish-speaking father. Or Spanglish with an Enniscorthy accent which would surely qualify as a new dialect. Once in the bodega on the corner I asked for razor blades and was given flypaper. And I was so proud of my Spanish!

One Sunday morning last summer I was standing on top of Vinegar Hill and looking down on my hometown: Enniscorthy, County Wexford. I noticed how compact the town was, how an American town with a similar population would need three or four times as much space, and it dawned on me why I had always felt so at ease in Inwood. Both Inwood and Enniscorthy are squeezed, compact, warm, and comfortable. To grow up in a small close-knit Irish country town is a good preparation for life in a New York neighborhood. In both you are part of your neighbors' lives: You smell their food, hear them making love. In Nebraska, where rugged individualism is favored over gentle communality, you are separated from your neighbors. Consequently, the day-by-day culture is often conducted in monosyllables or at a distance: We speak across fences or over the buzz of snowblowers.

🌀

When I arrived in Nebraska, one day I took my kids to Memorial Park at a time when I felt that other children would be playing there. But it was empty; there was no need to be out under a hot sun since houses have backyards and the streets are quiet enough for playing. Now there are no opportunities for me to sit down outdoors on neutral ground with neighbors and strangers, to enter into their lives, hear their stories, and learn some more about America. There are no fire hydrants turned on for kids to run through. And in the beginning, I sensed that people didn't want to talk to me, didn't need to know my story. However, because I didn't go away people have opened their arms, offered food in their houses, conversation, and friendship. Still, this is a more formal world which requires invitations for dinner, the checking of calendars, the cleaning-up of houses, and the elaborate preparation of food. There's no middle ground of park or bar where parents and children can hang out and let their guards down, where the grownups can play like their kids. Although I can relax with friends, I still long for the casual informality of the chat on the street. Sitting on the benches in Inwood Park, listening to the voices of mothers and children, I was so aware of the swish of great trees of the park, of the screeching of brakes on the parkway and bridge, and of the insistent, welcoming songs of the Hudson and Harlem rivers. The nearest I have come to reexperiencing such communality has occurred after heavy snowfalls when we gather in the park, close to the war memorial, and lunge, screaming, downhill on sleds.

It's difficult to socialize with people my own age, as most are locked into fixed ideas of family and parenthood, both of which preclude having a few drinks in a bar on a regular basis or coffee in a diner. I believe my neighbors should get out more, to spend more time with young adults, to abandon their television sets and fixed ideas. I look out the front window of my house at the bright sidewalks on which no one walks and experience an intense loneliness. The prairie is lonely and vast, and far from the ocean. Yet, as Kathleen Norris has pointed out in *Dakota: A Spiritual Geography*, it too is wondrous and a gifted teacher. Slowly, I open to it, learn its language, and enter into its mysteries. My kids have settled in to roam the alleyways behind the houses and claim the comfort of their block, and nothing gives me more pleasure than to press my face against the window and watch them roll about each winter in the snow.

I live in the city, not a suburb, but I think that after living in New York most other American cities will seem suburban to me. Fifteen months after we left Inwood we returned for a day and neither of my kids recognized our old apartment building. If I hadn't been there to point it out, they'd have walked right past it. This devastated me because I felt I'd pulled them out of childhood violently, and I feared, or even knew, that they would never have that strong sense of place I so deeply profess, that they had begun this impossible process of forgetting much sooner than I had, and that moving from the source of early experience had damaged them.

The other day I was listening to a pizza advert on the radio and the speaker claimed that now you could get New York-style pizza here in the "Heartland" without having to put up with New York-style rudeness and attitudes, and I thought to myself that they could keep their pizza—just let me have one slice of that rudeness and attitude for old times' sake. When my kids get cheeky, I don't complain too much—I say to myself, "They can't help it, they're New Yorkers," and I sit back and enjoy the banter. But I like where I live now, like being able to get out into the country in a few minutes, though I feel very strongly that when I left Inwood, I left home. And it bothers me that shouting at people on the phone gets me no respect here; it has taken the fun out of being hassled. Sometimes I suspect that people have trouble distinguishing rudeness from style. But I know I have settled and am happy. When I am away from here, I look forward to returning, and I long for those Nebraskans from whom I have learned what it means to be generous.

Four

Reading Mary Gordon's Final Payments *in America*

Before coming to live in the United States, I lived in that vast country through books, music, and the rich visual images presented in the movies I watched in Dublin cinemas. I was enthralled by the diverse products of the American imagination, by a world which seemed larger and more vital to me than what was available at home. In the 1970s, the decade when I made the transition from secondary school to college to the world of work, much of Irish writing exhibited a narrow thematic focus and a predictable realist style, while Irish popular music and cinema had yet to make their great leaps forward. The American artistic scene, on the other hand, was so diverse as to appear limitless. I left in 1982 and by the end of that decade and the beginning of the next, the arts in Ireland, and Irish society in general, had transformed themselves and, in the process, become outward looking, popular, and a vital area of operation which was viewed enviously by fellow artists and commentators from around the world. Very quickly, the Ireland I had known dissolved. This transformation is a delight because it has allowed me to put my earlier misgivings aside. Although the pace of change has seemed rapid, it is something which had been evolving for quite a while. Through newspapers, magazines, books, readings, and records, one knew a good deal about such artists as Neil Jordan, Dermot Bolger, and U2. What impressed me, as much as the various talents of these, and other, emerging figures, was that each allied quiet confidence and determination with charm and ease. These artists did not feel inferior or inadequate, as Irish artists had in the past. They were interested in getting on with their work, primarily, and Ireland seemed ready to accept them, and the world ready to embrace them. Although each has retained a distinctive Irish voice and emerged from a definite Irish cultural tradition, each has also pushed at the boundaries of the Irish artistic enterprise. As a result, Irish artists now take risks with subject matter and technique so we are allowed to see the experience of the Irish, at home and abroad, through new lenses. Indeed, the country itself has changed: To return to Ireland in the late 1990s after a significant absence, as I have done, is such an exciting event. I am returning to a new country, which addresses me in a new language I have had to learn.

I decided to come to America to follow the perfume left by books, movies, and albums. I arrived with a head full of images which I have tried to retain during my years here, though it has not always been easy or even desirable: images gleaned from Whitman and Twain, Cather and Kerouac, Stafford and Fitzgerald, Joni Mitchell and Tillie Olsen, Terence Malick and Peter Bogdanovich, which had seemed so full of difference and romance. My image of America in 1982 was one top-heavy with dynamism and long roads connecting sacred earths with teeming cities. America was a river of life where, at the end of the day and the driving, I would find a bright neon sign, a quiet bar, a glorious jukebox, and friendly patrons speaking in a variety of languages. America is so vast and complex that I have found all that I had imagined I would find. However, I have also come to realize the extent to which my vision was naive. In Dublin on St. Patrick's Day, we always laughed about the foolishness of Irish Americans who had crossed the Atlantic to march in the parade— their outlandish plaids, their ridiculous enthusiasm for an Ireland that was unknown to us natives. After a few years in America, it dawned on me that my own understanding of my new place was equally faulty. Yet it is difficult and inadvisable for both Irish Americans and myself to let go of the romance of place as it sheathes our visions and keeps our hopes warm. The romance of place can be a movable feast frequently looking beyond childhood and the present to the future.

Moving to New York in 1984, I discovered ethnic American writing, and it qualified, improved, and disproved the vision of America I had developed in Ireland. I went through the writings of Bernard Malamud and Isaac Bashevis Singer, Julia Alvarez and Anzia Yezierska. More slowly have I come to read the work of Irish American writers. I suspect that the reasons for this have more to do with my own anxieties than with misgivings I entertained about the books themselves. The longer I have lived in America, the more certain has become the fact of my permanent residence here, recent legislation enacted in Washington notwithstanding. I live in America, and my reluctance to read Irish American writing was, I suspect, an effort at denial. To read Irish America is to read about the self I have become, though I still cling to the notion that I am Irish and living in America. For a long time, I have embraced the notion of not belonging— of following American culture and politics as an outsider. In this way, I am as up-to-date on current events as any citizen, but, at the same time, I have had no desire to trade in my green card for citizenship, for the right to vote. In Ireland, being raised in an intensely political culture, I grew weary of having to produce opinions on historical and political issues, of collective belonging, and looked forward to the opportunities for distance and not having to belong which America offered. Also, I have resisted Irish American writing as I felt for a long time that America's most vital creative energies came from bohemian and ethnic America, which Irish America, by virtue of economic advancement and the election of Kennedy, has felt it has risen above.

In the long run, notions such as these are untenable unless tested against experience and reading of books. Given that political opinion and action have grown increasingly hostile to immigrants, it is rather immoral for me, as a breadwinner and taxpayer, to observe but not vote. Also, to stand outside Irish America is to deny both its complexity, energy, and considerable achievement and who I have become. Ambivalence is a postmodern condition, but it is, or at least it should be, secondary to faith and commitment. More than anything else, parenthood has taught me the limits of ambivalence, because being a parent is concerned with the personal, cultural, and political future. One cannot be ambivalent about one's own flesh and blood. One should not be ambivalent about one's fellow human beings.

As part of this process of living and maturing, I have come to the fiction, stories, and essays of Mary Gordon. Like Malamud, Singer, and Alvarez, she is concerned with individuals and families in conflict who have carried over values from the Old World and Caribbean, but who are forced into confusing negotiations and compromises with American secular culture. In much of Gordon's work, the grandparents and parents are allied with the parish and church while the younger offspring contest these traditional allegiances when they discover the possibilities offered by the world beyond parish, classroom, and neighborhood. Gordon understands the confusion of the older people, but she is also deeply aware of how badly the young have been trained—by family, institution, and turf—for life in America as it has unfolded since the 1960s. Ill-prepared by upbringing for making choices, Gordon's characters are forced by trial and error to learn how to live in greater America. Her work, in scope and style, will be familiar to readers of Irish fiction, as it is eerily aligned with the fiction written by Edna O'Brien, John McGahern, William Trevor, and Brian Moore, senior Irish writers who emerged in the 1950s and 1960s with visions of the Irish family which were as startling as they were fresh.

At one point in *Final Payments* (1978), Gordon's first novel, Isabel Moore tells Liz, her friend since childhood, the following:

> I want a terrific pair of high-heeled shoes, and a lipstick, so I can make noise on the sidewalk with my heels and put on lipstick like Rosalind Russell. Then I want a very small apartment, and I want people to refer to me as a bachelorette. (93)

This declaration comes at a defining moment in her life. After tending to her ailing father for eleven years, she has been freed by his death to return to the world and pick up the threads of her long-abandoned life. Her father was an educated, narrow-minded, conservative Catholic intellectual in love with doctrine who declared that the Catholic Church presented a superior faith: "[F]or my father, the refusal of anyone in the twentieth century to become part of the Catholic Church was not pitiable; it was malicious and willful" (4). He supported the South in the Civil War and General Franco in Spain, and blamed Voltaire and Rousseau "for the mess of the twentieth century" (4). His funeral was "full of priests" who, while he was alive, had come to seek his wisdom and guidance. It is clear from the start that Isabel loved him deeply as a father, and for his long-term commitment to an ideal. Isabel's eleven-year hiatus from the world to care for him testifies to her love but also to a kind of self-sacrifice that seems, perhaps, perverse and unhealthy. How are we to read this? Is it the result of an all-consuming love? Or is it a penitential gesture to repay God and her father for catching her in bed with her father's favorite student? Is it a respectable way to avoid having to deal with the world on an everyday basis? Or is it Gordon's illustration of the secondary role women have been forced to play in Irish American Catholic families? Isabel, the woman, must give up career and the possibility of her own personal fulfillment to tend to the needs of her father, the man. *Final Payments* is such a complex novel, on many levels, that inevitable questions such as these, though certainly posed, are not easily answered. They cannot be, because Isabel's life is a continuum driven by the present though rooted in the pains and glories of the past.

After her father's coffin had been lowered into the ground, Isabel understood that "she would have to invent an existence" for herself (5). Gordon's tracing of Isabel Moore's reinvention of self is a central focus of the novel and is by turns hilarious, exciting, frightful, and sad, but always beautifully rendered and very moving. The world Isabel left has been replaced, so she must enter a marketplace without the tools necessary to negotiate a way through it. Like a child lacking experience, she is forced to learn by trial and error. As she makes her mistakes, we feel that she should think and listen more before acting, but we also know that she has been cut off from experience for so long that she is hungry for it. As a Catholic, she has entered a post-Vatican II world which has replaced an inward-looking Latin church with an outward-looking ecumenism: The language of the mass has become the language of the street.

Economically and educationally, Irish Americans have made the great leap forward from the neighborhood to the suburb, and from the factory floor to the college classroom. The Kennedy presidency gave Irish Americans a sense of equality. Given the opportunities for education, employment, and upward mobility and the possibility of owning beautiful objects presented to Irish Americans in the 1960s, and the desirability in sharing in such a bounty, one can imagine them looking backward to the parish and neighborhood without regret. For this generation, the ancien regime must have seemed backward, out-of-touch, and undesirable. Of course, after migration to suburbia and assimilation had killed the provenance of the parish, Irish American intellectuals would mourn its demise. Such a view, however, represents nothing more than the nostalgia of the arrived. In nineteenth-century Ireland, people abandoned the Irish language in order to survive, and who can blame them? In the process, they did not become less Irish. Similarly, prosperity has not made Irish Americans less Irish American. What has happened is that they have redefined who they are. Isabel's father is a hero of the past and celebrated by priests and by his daughter as such, but his world has died with him. For Isabel, the difficulty of making the transition from the neighborhood in Queens to contemporary America is heightened by her eleven-year absence from contemporary America in a defining period of its development—during a long moment when it was re-creating itself.

At a deep level, Isabel understands these shifts that have taken place and wants to take her place in an exciting new world, and she moves swiftly. Why does she move with such speed to get away from Queens? In a wonderful essay on American fiction, "Good Boys and Dead Girls," Gordon suggests why Isabel moves with such alacrity:

> The story of America is the story of the escape from fate. Europeans crossed the ocean in order to be free of it; the movement from the small town to the city is a move out of the grip of fate. The freedom and autonomy that America is meant to stand for is the attempt to define the self outside the bruising authority of fate. (6)

When Isabel meets with John Delaney, her lawyer and old family friend, to settle her father's estate, she is confronted with her fate, at least as it is seen by others. In quick succession, he suggests she consider a career as a secretary, teacher, nurse, or paid companion, and these suggestions, especially the final two, fill Isabel with "nausea." For the rest of her life, she is fated to become like Margaret Casey, her father's embittered housekeeper. What Delaney fails to understand, in his quickness to stereotype her, is the depth of Isabel's independence, learned ironically from her father, and her social, economic, and intellectual superiority to Margaret. In preparation for her father's death and the new set of circumstances that this would bring about, Isabel had taken long walks on Sunday mornings instead of attending mass. On her way home from Delaney's office, she buys *Vogue* and then goes shopping in Bloomingdale's with her friend Eleanor. Delaney identifies Isabel with her sacrifice to her father. He assumes that such devotion indicates that repeating such sacrifices represents the modus operandi of her life. However, Isabel's eleven years were given up to one man only, and now that he's dead she wishes to resume her life. She was not made to be separated from the world and none of her complex desires have been lessened by time.

Isabel shares much with Judy Hearne, the protagonist of another first novel, Brian Moore's *The Lonely Passion of Judith Hearne* (1955). But Judy, who has also devoted many years to taking care of an ailing parent, emerges into a rigid society in Belfast which refuses to allow her escape from her designation as spinster. In addition, she lacks Isabel's youth, looks, money, friends, and education. Mary Gordon is ambivalent when it comes to the American notion of freedom. She understands that, until recently, this has resulted in women having to occupy a secondary place in history, and she is, instead, drawn to the notion of neighborhood and its promise of equal shelter, on an ideal level at least. But while it is possible for Isabel to leave because American society permits such escapes, post-World War II Belfast will not allow Judy Hearne such a route, and as a consequence, she finds shelter in alcohol and delusion. Isabel leaves Queens to escape her fate. Isabel's flight also contains echoes of Cait's in Edna O'Brien's trilogy; in fact, *Final Payments* seems a distillation of this theme whereas *The Country Girls Trilogy* is an elaboration.

On another level, Isabel's decision to sell her house and leave the old neighborhood in Queens for good is an archetypal Irish fable which continues the diaspora of the race which began in rural Ireland in the distant past, and which has been renewed, if this is the right word, by the migration away from the parish to the city or suburb. Isabel's progress is not completely smooth. She is able to find a job and renew friendships with old friends, but two affairs with married men turn out badly, and she is so humiliated by the wife of the second that she briefly abandons the world to live with Margaret Casey, her father's embittered former housekeeper, and a woman Isabel despises. Eventually, her friends Eleanor and Liz bring her back into the world. It is clear that the movement away from the parish island can be as full of trauma as the earlier departure from the island of Ireland. Also, to grow up in an island culture (whether the real one in Ireland or the more metaphorical version in Queens), for all its pleasures, leaves the man and woman somewhat unprepared for mainland life. And to return is not an option. At certain times in history, one must leave familiar ground in order to escape fate. Irish people fleeing famine understood this well.

Edna O'Brien has described the language of *The Country Girls Trilogy* as being "very natural" (Carlson, 71). The language of *Final Payments* is also equally natural in tone and it is quite an achievement on Gordon's part to have been able to accommodate so well the deeply resonant themes with the simplicity of language. Also of note—and this is a delightful aspect of the novel—is Gordon's ability to provide comic relief. My favorite example of this is Isabel's comment, when asked to decide which kind of contraception she wants to use, "I knew about the diaphragm: I had read Mary McCarthy" (106). Of course, such comedy is also a reminder of Isabel's wide and independent reading.

Gordon's memoir of her father, *The Shadow Man* (1996), is a book that works well in tandem with *Final Payments* and some of her other books. In his devotion to Catholicism and to his daughter, David Gordon is reminiscent of Isabel Moore's father in *Final Payments*. However, he is also forced to make choices similar to those made by Isabel. As Gordon's narrative unfolds, we wonder why David Gordon abandoned Judaism for Catholicism, why he lied to his daughter about his early life to make it much more impressive than it actually was, and why he'd become an arch-conservative and an anti-Semite. David Gordon reinvented himself, more than once, and he did so to escape from an undistinguished background and a social and economic climate unfavorable to Jews. He is a Gatsby-like figure whose desire to be considered important ends in disappointment. America, by nature of its size and outlook, allows for such reinventions. Individual and collective memory, so vital in the parish and village, can be put aside in the melting pot. For the immigrant from Ireland or elsewhere, the possibility of forgetting a hungry past makes America the land of opportunity. Of course, it is far from certain that reinvention will lead to happiness, and as Fitzgerald makes clear, society will not always accommodate the individual's desire to be free of his or her individual history. But Isabel Moore does not seek to escape her Irishness; she instead adapts it for secular, contemporary America, as contemporary America adapts to accommodate her.

In *The Other Side* (1989), Gordon explores the lives of two Irish immigrants, Ellen and Vincent McNamara, and their offspring. Charles

Fanning has called the representation of the Irish in the novel "mean-spirited" and "a blanket indictment of a people" (510). The McNamaras are certainly an exhausted family. Both the elderly patriarch and matriarch have been unwell, and their children have grown into confused and undistinguished adults who are to gather at the family home to await the homecoming of Vincent McNamara from a convalescent home. As a novel, it will remind the reader of Elizabeth Cullinan's *House of Gold* (1970), though, for all its length and elaboration, *The Other Side* is not as effective as Cullinan's brief book. It's hardly "a blanket indictment of a people," though. More accurately, it is a rather long-winded exploration of the sort of unhappy family that has long been in the forefront of Irish and Irish American writing.

Mary Gordon has not restricted herself to writing about Irish Americans. In fact, from reading *Men and Angels* (1985) and the three superb novellas comprising *The Rest of Life* (1993), one could hardly guess that Gordon is Irish American. This fact points to the essential difference between the Irish and Irish American writer of fiction. Whether the Irish writer is writing about Doolin, London, or Missoula, she or he is always an Irish writer. However, the Irish American writer must write on some recognizably Irish American theme for his or her novel to be considered Irish American. If a writer does not write about Irish Americans, as Gordon does in *The Rest of Life,* he or she will be labeled an American writer. The problem for an Irish American writer is that the field of operation is rather small, but if he or she abandons this field, there will no longer be an Irish American novel, unless the parameters are extended. When she writes on non-Irish American themes, Gordon's fiction becomes more daring technically as she uses the freedoms allowed by the larger canvas. Other writers, Michael Stephens and Thomas McGonigle in particular, have used postmodern techniques to provide old material with fresh life. And in recent times, new arrivals from Ireland like Colum McCann and Emer Martin have come with hybrid imaginations to create some remarkable work. One sees in Irish American writing much excellent individual work, and one waits for the great, collective leap forward to match what is currently happening in Ireland. One sees clear advances being made in music and film, and so one wonders whether a great rebirth is already under way.

Over the years, I've tried to get around America as much as possible. However, since I can't go everywhere, I've relied on writers to do much of my exploring for me. Truthfully, the parish world of Irish American

Catholics didn't interest me that much when I arrived because it reeked of familiarity and because I did not seek to replicate my experience of Ireland in America. The last thing I wanted to do was to go to a church social or bingo session, or hear musicians playing jigs and reels. But time has brought me around to a more reasoned understanding, and a sense of belonging to Irish America. What have I learned from Mary Gordon? *Final Payments,* in particular, strikes me as being a very important examination of an Irish America in the process of change, wrought from within and without, from one way of seeing to another—with the father representing the old and the daughter the new. As I have pointed out, the road ahead is difficult. Gordon, in this novel and in many of her other works, displays a great ability to detail and explore the painful choices which younger Irish Americans have had to make. Also, she understands the difficulties people face when they have to navigate between cultures and places, and she shows that for the Irish the process of migration continues long after they have left their native places.

Five

Four Paintings by Danny Maloney
A Short Story

The four paintings hanging on the walls in the Goldstein Gallery made no sense to me on opening night, but neither did any of the others by the rest of the artists who were part of the show. I looked at Danny Maloney's and nodded my head at what caught my eye, or at something I recognized—like the odd lavender curtains and sheets in a hotel room, at the East River and the Brooklyn Bridge. When I noticed his ring in the corner of one painting, I looked closer and found the shape of his hand buried under newspaper. A hole had been slit in the newspaper, big enough for me to see the ring on the little finger of his left hand, his drinking hand. The downtown crowd distracted me: shrieking, hugging, calling, waving, and talking loudly about each other's doings and what they would do afterward. "Are you going on to the opening down the street?" a woman asked me. They fascinated me: I wandered about eavesdropping on their small talk and studying their clothes—bought at Bergdorf's, estate sales, Goodwill. Scarves and black cowboy boots were in.

I was also thinking of my husband at home, way uptown in the Inwood Section, putting the children to bed, laughing to myself: What a lark he'd have looking at this crowd. It didn't faze me that I knew no one. Of course, seeing Danny Maloney's paintings connected me to the opening, gave me a reason to be here. But Danny wasn't present; there was no set of blue eyes telling me I had to say something smart. I don't need to do that anymore. I talk to my family now, and to my first-grade class in the school on Vermileya Avenue—the school with bars on the windows, chains on the doors, and a security man in a chair at the door who directs all visitors to the office. My life in my home neighborhood. New York City.

Grace Maloney told me about the exhibition, that she'd gotten a letter and a catalogue from the gallery. She wrote and said she'd asked the gallery to invite me to the opening since I was the only person she knew in

New York except for her cousins on Seaman Avenue, and they wouldn't be interested in going anyway. I was still angry with her for not telling me about what had happened to Danny, for not even telling me he was sick so I could have visited him. She said no one knew until he was dead. I never believed her: Grace always knows. She spent her life tracking his every move. Her brother! A year later, one Saturday morning in the playground in Inwood while the children were digging in the sandbox, she told me the story. She said that when he died she and her parents had come to New York and spent a weekend in an apartment down the street from me. She hadn't called. The Irish family: It draws you in, then it shuts you out. Standing together against the world.

I set aside another day to see the paintings. One Saturday, my husband came downtown with me on the train. I left him at the Canal Street station with the boys and gave him the following instructions: to walk around Chinatown showing them the produce stands, the fish, and the live crabs in the white buckets. When they got hungry, there was a McDonald's on Canal. Buy each of them a toy from the street vendors. He said he'd also bring them to Canal Jeans on Broadway to look for T-shirts. I told him I'd be at 580 Broadway, that I'd meet him at the coffee shop on the corner in three hours.

Grace on the park bench, drinking soda that day had said: "We took a taxi in from the airport to the hospital and went upstairs and sat in a room and a black woman asked us whether we wanted coffee, where we were after coming from, were we tired. The folks said nothing. Daddy hadn't said a word since we'd got the news, and Mammy only spoke to me when Daddy was gone. I was thinking to myself how weird it was— to be in New York in a hospital called St. Vincent's, just like at home, and with the holy pictures on the walls, the crucifixes, and the pictures of John Paul II everywhere."

"In the Village," I told her.

"With the bags piled in the corner, not being able to smoke. And it was so quiet. You couldn't hear the traffic on the street. The freezing air flowing through the room, even though it was scorching outside."

"It's a famous hospital," I said, "where Dylan Thomas died. That's where the boys were born."

The first painting I looked at is called "Stones." In the center of the canvas stand a bunch of gray boulders. Above them the sky is mostly gray too, though a lighter gray than the stones, and with patches of fluffy white here and there. In circles around the stones are rows of pebbles, then tufts of grass, then deep green grass. No figures. An Irish landscape? What does it mean? Of course, when I looked back on it I guessed that this first painting was an Irish scene to tell people that Danny Maloney was Irish. The painting was as cold as Danny was when he talked about Ireland, or "home," as he spitefully called it. When you think of Ireland, you are supposed to think of the green fields. But you could just as easily think of the stones and the rocks you see everywhere. Stones that are the color of the weather, representing Irish silences: the man from Carlow I fell in love with who couldn't hold me when I felt weak, who could never say the words I needed to hear. One year was enough there. I'm glad I didn't stay. The grass at the edges of this painting is a drug. It's like heroin—calming, deflective, warming the stones. But the cold gray stone—cold and strong—is Ireland. Is the man standing at his front door, smoking his pipe, smiling at you? His shiny clothes. His nodding wife making cups of tea.

"It's time for the *News,* Charlie," I hear her call.

"After an age," Grace said, "the door opened and two men came in. My father looked at the floor. I stood up. One man said he was sorry for our grief or something odd like that and then said, 'Here's the death certificate. Mr. O'Brien will help with the other details.' And he walked out. I looked at Mr. O'Brien. A man in his forties wearing a sports coat and a pair of gray trousers, like anyone you'd meet at home. He looked at us all. I smiled. Mammy nodded. Daddy said nothing; he just dug his hands into the arms of the chair the same way as he'd dug them into the side of his seat on the plane. Daddy who'd always wanted to come to America. Mr. O'Brien sat down and took a folder from his case. He said: 'Danny Maloney was a good friend of mine. A good friend of many in our community in New York. When people got sick, he visited them. That was his way of helping. When he got sick, we took care of him. Friends brought him his meals, bathed him, changed his sheets, helped him with his bills. In the hospital, one of us was always here to hold his hand. Up to the end. We wanted him to get in touch with you, but he said we shouldn't—he was worried about what you'd say if you saw him.' He sighed and looked at me. 'I have his will,' he said. 'He asked me to sell his possessions and donate the money to an organization here in the city which helps people who get sick. Some of his paintings will be exhibited next year and the proceeds . . .' He stopped."

The second painting was the largest on display. "Immigrants" is its title, and it is divided into distinct panels. The viewer follows it from left to right. In the first panel, a mass of people is seen walking on the Brooklyn Bridge in the direction of Manhattan. They are holding banners and placards. You cannot see a face or make out what's written. You see blurs and lines. But the gray sky and water are clearly visible. The second focuses on the deep black faces of the marchers. They are Haitians. In the third panel are some cops standing on the sidewalk, watching the marchers. They have that bored look you see on the faces of all the officers of the NYPD. In the final panel, a man is on a platform speaking into a microphone outside Federal Plaza. I remember this march, when thousands of Haitians walked from Brooklyn to the offices of the Immigration and Naturalization Service calling for an end to discrimination against them. They did not deserve to be punished for the presence of AIDS in this country. The marchers are bright, colorful, and noble in the painting; the rest of the world is drab. Politics! Something Danny Maloney never cared about. Or maybe just Irish politics. But when you're gay in America today, and an immigrant, you're involved in politics whether you like it or not. This is a more hopeful painting than "Stones." Danny looks at the Caribbean people and loves them in a way he can't love the Irish, his own people. They're exotic. I remember seeing a video on MTV of U2. They were singing with a black choir in Harlem. Can't remember the song. Maybe it was "I Still Haven't Found What I'm Looking For." They come to America, embrace the downtrodden, and leave. It does Bono's ego some good, but that's about it. I teach the children of men and women who have died of AIDS: shooting up, fucking, dying. Each day. But I'm happy with Danny Maloney when I think of him bringing food to a sick man's house, holding the hand of a dying friend in St. Vincent's, Poor Clare's, or at St. Luke's. Sickness and loneliness changed his life. Bono goes home first-class; Danny travels in the cargo hold.

Danny Maloney. One night when I was a student in Dublin Grace brought you along to Mulligan's. You told me all about the New York I cared little about—the museums, the galleries, life in the Village. You knew them better than I who had seen them without ever caring for them. My world: Inwood, Good Shepherd Church and School, Bronx Science, Fordham University. Going downtown to eat, shop, and see the movies, entering enemy territory. I spent a year in Ireland because I won a scholarship my father insisted I apply for: He thought it would be good for me to "experience" his homeland. I prefer the Bronx Irish to the New Ross Irish. Danny Maloney told me he wanted to live in New York.

"Daddy looked up. 'What are ye saying this for,' his voice hoarse and breaking. 'He's dead. We don't know you. Who sent you to talk to us?'

'Danny, Mr. Maloney . . .' 'Maybe you didn't hear me. We don't want you here. Isn't that right, Joan?' My mother said, 'It would be better if you left us alone.' I told him I'd talk with him. We went to another room, but I didn't know what to say. I was thinking of the cheek of that fella coming to the hospital and confronting us like that. It was only making things worse for us all. Like it was a conspiracy. He asked me whether I wanted any of Danny's personal effects. I said I didn't. Did we want to see the body? I went and asked Daddy. He said: 'All the arrangements are taken care of. We are taking the body home on Sunday. Now tell that man to get out of our sight.' That was it then: We had until tomorrow to wait to get the plane home."

She didn't want any of her brother's personal effects! Imagine that! Why? Whenever he was home Danny and his father went fishing together. They came home happy, smelling of beer. I remember the two of them laughing together in the yard as they cleaned the fish. The family that adopted me in Ireland, that invited me down the country.

The third painting is called "Home." A young man is caught in the act of taking off his T-shirt. His head is covered by it, his back is deeply tanned. The bed sheets and curtains are lavender. Outside under a gray sky you can see the Empire State Building. Danny Maloney is sitting on a chair watching. You can't see him in the painting, but you can see his ring through a slit in *The New Ross Standard,* which is open on the table in front of him. To live as he wanted to is why he came to America, to my back door. One night in his parents' house he came to my room and we made love. What, I wonder, would the Maloneys have thought, if Mr. O'Brien had not come to see them in the hospital?

Danny Maloney's funeral? "Sad, but beautiful," his sister told me. A sunny August morning in New Ross. Heartbreaking when the young are taken away, I imagine the priest saying. The truth is lost.

"That night we had the relative's apartment to ourselves; they were called away suddenly. We ate our dinner and watched television until it was time to go to bed. The next morning we went on the subway to St. Patrick's Cathedral to mass. We saw the spires when we got out of the station, but when we got up close to it there were police and barricades everywhere and a huge crowd roaring and shouting and cursing."

"An Act Up and Queer Nation demonstration," I said.

"The police cleared a way through the crowd for the people going to mass, but the crowd was shouting at us. Daddy was jostled, and white in the face. Can you imagine it, after all he'd been through? When the cardinal was giving his sermon, they started shouting at him. The police came and took them away. Then, during the Communion, they got the hosts and spit them out on the altar."

She went on like this. I continued to look across the playground to the sandbox, then to the slides when the boys moved over there to play. This my park, I was thinking to myself, close to the two rivers, the boathouse, and oak trees.

"After the mass, we collected our bags from the apartment and took a taxi to the airport. I remember it was 3:00 P.M. when we got there, hours before the plane was due to leave. And it was there that Daddy took to crying."

"It was too late," I said.

She looked at me.

"And what about yourself?" I asked.

"I think of him."

🌀

The last painting is entitled "Why I Like the Prairie." Under an enormous sky is a cornfield, one which has already been harvested. The stalks stick up at odd angles from the earth, turning brown. The earth is black. There are no figures: no people, no cars. Whenever I am reminded of desolation, of being heartbroken and lonely, I hear Randy Travis's voice, in which all of our griefs are harbored. I have this vision of him in my soul on a vast concert tour filling football stadiums with all of my brothers and sisters. After the concert concludes, they drive off into the darkness, tears drying on their faces, but possessed of the powers of description. There is nothing on the prairie; that's why it frightens me. But my husband, I guess because he grew up in Kansas, likes it for just that reason; there you can get away from it all. For Danny Maloney, I guess, the attraction was the same. There was always too much of everything in Ireland (friends, family, history) and in New York (love, death, and people). Here there is nothing. I know you liked to withdraw. There's nothing on the prairie except yourself. And it is your prairie.

The boys were drinking soda in the café when I met them there. They shouted at me as I walked toward them and showed me their new Ninja Turtles. "Hey dudes and dudettes," they sang. My husband was drinking coffee. He smiled at me. In a way, I was glad I'd made this second trip downtown to see these paintings. I looked at my husband, "Hold me close tonight. Whisper over and over—I love you, I love you," I said with my eyes. He knew.

Six

The Search for Majestic Shades
Contemporary American Poets Migrate to Ireland

In the last decade or so, a number of American poets have fixed their gazes firmly on the Irish poetic and physical landscapes. Included in this group are Billy Collins, Janice Fitzpatrick-Simmons, Michael Heffernan, Ben Howard, Anne Kennedy, Sabra Loomis, Thomas Lynch, Ted McNulty, R. T. Smith, and Richard Tillinghast, who join Jessie Lendennie, Julie O'Callaghan, and Knute Skinner, long-standing permanent or semi-permanent residents of Ireland. In addition, the poet Jean Valentine spent a number of years as a semi-permanent Irish resident. Given the ease, if not the comfort, of air travel, the availability of grants, and the perception that Ireland is in the midst of a cultural rebirth, it seems likely that this trend will continue in the future. After I examine this phenomenon, both through the lens of history and through the words of the poets themselves, I will conclude that this trans-Atlantic traffic is, and will continue to be, important and enriching for both Irish and Irish American poetry.

We shouldn't assume, however, that these are the first American poets in recent times to discover Ireland. In a letter written to Thomas McGreevy dated January 27, 1949, Wallace Stevens noted that "Rome is not ordinarily on the itinerary of my imagination. It is a little out of the way, covered by cypresses. It is not a place one visits frequently like Paris or Dublin." The Irish literary renaissance and the works of James Joyce put Ireland in the minds of many writers, from Jorge Luis Borges in Buenos Aires to Wallace Stevens in Hartford. One of Stevens's most remarkable later poems was inspired by a postcard photo of the Cliffs of Moher:

> They go to the Cliffs of Moher rising out of the mist,
> Above the real,
>
> Rising out of the present time and place, above
> The wet, green grass.

This is not landscape, full of the somnambulations
Of poetry

And the sea. This is my father or, maybe,
It is as he was,

A likeness, one of the race of fathers: earth
And sea and air.

"The Irish Cliffs of Moher," *Collected Poems*, 501–502

But Stevens wrote of Ireland from a distance: It was a country explored through letters, books, and visual images which fed his imagination. While his friends and correspondents traveled throughout Europe, Stevens remained in Hartford working as a lawyer and executive for an insurance company; however, the close contact he maintained with friends who could travel allowed Stevens to be present imaginatively in Europe, and these contacts influenced both what and how he wrote. His friendship with McGreevy, the Irish poet and the director of the National Gallery in Dublin, enabled Stevens to fully engage his interest in Ireland. "The Irish Cliffs of Moher" was inspired by a postcard of the cliffs sent to him by another friend, Jack Sweeney. In addition to the poem, the card elicited the following comment from Stevens (in a letter to Barbara Church):

> Jack Sweeney (the Boston Sweeney) sent me a post-card from County
> Clare the other day—worn cliffs towering up over the Atlantic. It was a
> great gust of freedom, a return to the spacious, solitary world in which we
> used to exist. . . . (*Letters*, 760–61)

Like Yeats and Synge, Stevens leaves the problematic contemporary world and enters an ancient Irish landscape which speaks a wild and spacious language. What is interesting about Stevens's attachment to Ireland, in light of the current wave of American poets who have followed him, is that he did not emerge from an Irish American background and so such concerns as contemporary Irish politics, family, religion, and the diaspora are generally outside his range of interest. It is the literary and physical esthetic which draws him to Ireland, and also the notion, which Stevens felt strongly, that in Ireland the imagination is allowed freer play. It is ironic, of course, given the pervasive censoring of creative work in Ireland in the 1940s and 1950s by the Irish Censorship Board, that Stevens would have chosen these decades to become interested in Ireland. In Ireland, the poems, fiction, and plays of the local maestros were generally seen in a negative light, and many Irish writers sought to come to the United States to earn a living and to escape the suffocating neo-puritanism of Ireland.

Whereas Stevens remained at home and imagined Ireland, the writers of the generation of poets that followed him set out for Ireland. In Robert

Lowell's work, Ireland is important. As a result of his marriage to Caroline Blackwood, he spent time in Ireland in the 1970s, and his 1977 collection *Day by Day* chronicles this marriage and its dissolution. As Ian Hamilton points out in his biography, Lowell spent his last night alive locked inside a wing of Castletown House in County Kildare. However, the most important figure in these trans-Atlantic transactions of this period is John Berryman, who composed the final book of his *Dream Songs*, Book Seven, in Dublin. The 106 poems which comprise this book are firmly rooted in Irish political and literary history, and Ireland, as John Montague has pointed out, was an enabling factor which facilitated Berryman's completion of his great work:

> For he seemed to me positively happy, a man who was engaged in completing his life's work, with a wife and child he adored. He had come into his own and radiated the psychic electricity of genius. (*The Figure in the Cave,* 202)

In *The Pressed Melodeon,* his recent collection of essays on modern Irish writing, Ben Howard lists a number of reasons why he and, by implication, other contemporary American poets and their predecessors have been drawn to Ireland. He notes that "it is heartening to visit an English-speaking country where the idea of a poet is taken seriously . . . and where one's language matters so much" (26–27), and he is drawn to a poetry whose "omphalos [life force] is almost always local" and not, as he believes is often the case in American poetry, an "inward location" (9). Howard is drawn to the tragic theme in Irish poetry, which also appealed to Berryman and which he articulated so well in "Dream Song 309":

> I went shopping today & came back with
> a book about the Easter Rising, reality & myth—
> all Henry's old heroes,
> The O'Rahilly, Plunkett, Connolly, & Pearse,
> spring back into action, fatuous campaigners
> dewy with phantastic hope.
>
> Phantastic hope rules Henry's war as well,
> all these enterprises are doomed, all human pleas
> are headed for the night.
> Wait the lime-pits for all originators,
> wounded propped up to be executed,
> afterward known as martyrs.
>
> 331

Both Berryman and Howard admire the strength and flexibility of the Irish lyric which is able to give order and grace to complex social, political, personal, and artistic concerns. One senses in Howard's work as a critic an impatience with much of the confessional excesses of American poetry, which have narrowed the range of a once broad, national voice. But in Ireland, there is a sense of a continuum, albeit one, as both Howard and Eavan Boland point out, which continues to require prodding and redefinition. In *Object Lessons,* Eavan Boland describes her efforts to break away from the "male and bardic" formation of the Irish poem, in a struggle comparable to Adrienne Rich's in the United States:

> I was skeptical of the very structure of the Irish poem. Its inherited voice, its authoritative stance, its automatic reflex of elegy—these given qualities, from a technical perspective, accrued too much power to the speaker to allow that speaker to be himself a plausible critic of power. (191)

In common with Boland, many younger Irish poets, both female and male, look toward America and find in its poetry a means of escape from the strictures of the Irish lyric which, to many, is unsuited to contemporary conditions. These poets, too, like Joyce's Stephen Dedalus, seek to escape from the prison of history and to emerge into a bright, immediate world. In their recent collections, both Mary O'Donnell and Patrick Chapman celebrate the splendor of the American surface and employ distinctive American poetic forms. They find in American playfulness relief from the earnestness of Ireland and its stiff literary tradition. In "Spiderwoman's Third Avenue Rhapsody," O'Donnell describes "the pussy-suckers, the traders, the metropolitan chowder" (17) of Times Square and ends her poem in celebration of the artificial, which contrasts with the left-behind wholesomeness of the green fields of Ireland:

> this dreaming, ocean prominence,
> this violet, scandal-lit place,
> this beautiful fakery,
> O wild Manhattan! (*cresc. fff*)
>
>   18

O'Donnell's celebration of American fakery contrasts with Brian Moore's disgust as it is revealed in *The Great Victorian Collection.* Chapman is also drawn toward the urban New York light and away from its rural Irish counterpart:

> Forbidden to smoke in the apartment,
> I sit up on the roof and watch the trails of passing
>   aeroplanes
> And automobile streams of red and brilliant white on
>   Broadway.
>   "Night on 109th Street," 3

It is ironic, then, that American poets, tired of the abuse of freedom at home, have looked to Ireland for a more stable sense of poetic form. Among younger Irish poets, on the other hand, there exists a general feeling of awe at the American poetic achievement, from the modernists to the present.

Howard and his generation have been brought to Ireland as much by the pull of the poetic tradition as by ancestry; as he points out, Howard did not come from an Irish background. In fact, many of these poets, since they have no first-hand knowledge of it, bypass Irish America entirely. But their engagement with Irish writing is as urgent as Berryman's, which he expressed so well in "Dream Song 312," his address to Yeats:

> I have moved to Dublin to have it out with you,
> majestic Shade, You whom I read so well
> so many years ago,
> did I read your lesson right? did I see through
> your phases to the real? your heaven, your hell
> did I enquire properly into?
>
> 334

In "Dublin in July," Howard echoes Berryman's sentiments, though he has come to Dublin to enter into a discourse with Kavanagh's shade primarily:

> Mendacious Dublin, plying us with shades
> of Yeats, Behan, Kavanagh, O'Brien,
> inveigles us with drollery and squalor,
> heroic ghosts transformed, transmogrified
> by accident or craft. Remembered deeds . . .
>
> *Lenten Anniversaries*, 21

Both Lowell and Berryman wrote for an American audience, and their primary place of publication was America. What is notable and different about the current wave of poets is that they are publishing their collections in Ireland and seeking a primarily Irish readership. In recent times, Irish publishers of poetry have received more generous government subsidies, and this extra funding has allowed them to take a more international view of poetry; for them, to bend Kavanagh's dictum, the new Irish view of poetry must be parochial and international. Again, however, we must recognize that this development is not completely new but another continuum. In the 1960s and 1970s, Dolmen Press published collections of U.S.-born poets such as Knute Skinner and Thomas Dillon Redshaw, and Raven Arts Press published mainland European poets in translation in the 1970s and 1980s. Today, Dedalus has continued where Raven left off and frequently includes European translations on its list. These publishers, and Irish poets in general, have responded to Anthony Cronin's charge delivered from the pages of *The Bell* in 1953 that "we must look outward again or die, if only of boredom" (Brown, 227). Because there is more money available and a less insular view of poetry, Irish poetry lists have grown remarkably diverse and cosmopolitan in recent times.

An important publisher with regard to this current wave of migrant American poets is Jessie Lendennie of Salmon Publishing, a native of Arkansas and the publisher of most of the poets mentioned at the beginning of this chapter. In an essay on Salmon, Victor Luftig notes that the range of writers published "is of the type one may as readily associate with modernist Paris as with modern Ireland . . . and is matched by comparable diversity in gender, generation, style, and theme" (108). As Luftig points out, this internationalization of Irish poetry lists serves to confirm Richard Kearney's argument that "Ireland can no longer be contained within the frontiers of an island" and that Irish culture will be "enhanced rather than annihilated by contact with other cultures" (Luftig, 109). Of course, much of the experience of the Irish has taken place outside of Ireland, of which this current interest in internationalism is a belated recognition. Kearney is also concerned with the notion of the "migrant mind," one formed by contact with other regions, which will enrich Ireland. The poets who have come to Ireland from America are migrants in this regard whose books detail not just an interest in Ireland, but also engagements with other places, in America and elsewhere. In her collection *The Dog Kubla Dreams My Life* (1994), Anne Kennedy includes many Irish poems, but these she places alongside poems of upstate New York and California. An even more striking variety can be found in Ted McNulty's *On the Block* (1995), where the locations range from the Bronx to County Cavan and from St. Stephen's Green to Bali. Clearly, the poet's gaze can no longer be defined by one home or by one voyage, but by many homes and many voyages.

In the work of these American poets two concerns are paramount: One is sense of place and engagement with it, and the other is the sensation of simultaneously belonging in Ireland and being outside of it, though in rare instances all barriers are broken down. The form chosen to render these themes is, generally, the short lyric and the short line, forms mastered by Irish poets. In Knute Skinner's work, much of which is centered on the townland of Killaspuglonane, near Liscannor in County Clare, place is unequivocally celebrated time and time again:

> Seven o'clock and the early October sun
> has yet to appear on the Ennistymon hill.

Darkness eliminates the grass and stones,
but a kitchen light comes vaguely over the fields.
In the calm I hear the patient sound of cattle
as the morning advances on Killaspuglonane.

"October Morning," 4

Skinner is influenced by the early work of Kavanagh, but adds to this an often surrealistic range of association. In his quiet and elegant way, Skinner reveals in his work a radical dissatisfaction with America, not the one of his Midwestern childhood, but the divided America of the 1960s:

When we look back on the year of assassinations,
I'll remember this garden in Killaspuglonane.
In April, when Micky's horse had ploughed our field
and when Martin Luther King was murdered in Memphis,
we dug our grief into the broken soil,
forking manure into the furrows, spreading
potato seeds on the manure, and then
throwing up drills where old furrows had been.
With the broken shovel I sliced into the dirt
to make room for the long roots of cabbage plants.
An ocean away from Memphis we moved into May,
completing the garden with peas, carrots, lettuce,
swiss chard and vegetable marrow.
Throughout the accounts of the riots, through the
    world's rhetoric,
we had planted a garden far away from King's balcony,
far away from the funeral and those last, useless
    tributes.
But the news reminded us of how young he was;
and, oh my America, you had killed your young hero.

"April–June 1968," 19

In the quiet world of County Clare, Skinner finds both an escape from and an antidote to an America torn apart by political, racial, and economic division and recovers in some emotional form (in the fields which surround his cottage) "the certainties of childhood," to borrow a phrase of Malcolm Cowley's which he used to describe "the lost generation" (9).

To find his voice in his Irish poems, Ben Howard borrows the sonnet form from the later Kavanagh and adapts it to his designs. Howard's new book *Midcentury*, set in Dublin during the Second World War, forces us to consider the context in which it should be read. Its subject matter suggests that it can be more profitably read in tandem with Kavanagh's *Lough Derg* than with the work of an American poet. Howard believes that Irish and American poetry—the frontier and the bog, to use his and

Seamus Heaney's phrase—have much in common which facilitates the exchange between the two. The links between Ireland and America, however, are also thematic. Writing of the South in "from Sewanee in Ruins," Richard Tillinghast notes:

> History stopped in 1865,
> then started again as memory.
> *Today in the Café Trieste*, 86

If one were to change the date to 1798 or 1845, these lines could easily describe events in Ireland. Tillinghast, too, in a riff on a line from Ginsberg's *Howl*, reveals intense feelings of estrangement from America:

> "The best minds of *my* generation," too
> self-exiled from America,
> strangers to power,
> a wasted generation.
> *Today in the Café Trieste*, 75

But Ireland is restorative since it enables the poet to reenter the realm and spirit, if not the time and place, of a lost American childhood:

> And so do I—to drink in the presence
> Of these presences, these ideas given substance,
> Solid as your father's signature
> *A Quiet Pint in Kinvara*, 11

In the work of Ted McNulty and Janice Fitzpatrick-Simmons the dislocation of the migrant and the ironies of the journey are eloquently described. The work of both of these poets is of a high quality and merits close attention. For McNulty, there is a double exploration of dislocation—his father's in the Bronx and his own in County Cavan, where his father came from. His explorations of his father's exile bring to mind John Montague's work in *The Dead Kingdom* and Padraic Fiacc's in the autobiographical fragment which rounds out his volume of selected poems. In "Oaf and Idler," McNulty describes selling his father's house (which recalls the selling of the family house in Mary Gordon's *Final Payments*), and using the money to go to Ireland. In "The Immigrant," McNulty explores both his distance from and his proximity to the Irish world:

> The Yank in me
> rides the sound
> of loose chippings
> on a Cavan road,

> a neighbour
> taking me along
> to the cattle auction
> in a shed of wet coats
>
> where I'm a stranger
> in a ring of men
> but close to the creatures,
> smells old as straw.
>
> Driving back, the radio
> plays "California Blue"
> as I go in two directions,
> neither of them home
>
> While road stones crackle
> the hard words of immigrants,
> telling me now I must live
> in the cut of myself.
>
> *On the Block,* 45

The final lines echo Joyce's advice to Seamus Heaney in part 12 of *Station Island.*

Janice Fitzpatrick-Simmons's collection *Settler* (1995), is an elegant interweaving of the classic Irish lyric with the concrete and detailed New England lyric of Emily Dickinson and Donald Hall. Yet despite the sense of exhilaration evoked by the landscape of North Antrim, there is the recognition of distance between the poet and her Irish subjects:

> In exile, recalling the summer's heat,
> I've walked, collecting leaves and kindling,
> fall's silver, the threads of Fireweed,
> and this:
>
> a foreign place, our love, two homes.
>
> "I Dream I Lose America," 33

More than the other writers, Fitzpatrick-Simmons is able to juxtapose physical landscapes in such interesting ways, perhaps because she has brought a well-wrought literary and historical sense of the connection between nature and poetic form with her from New England to Ireland. Furthermore, her interest in the names of birds, flowers, shrubs, and her celebration of both the living things and the names they are known by brings to mind the world and methods of the ancient bardic poets. In her work (although she does certainly stress and examine the disjunction of experience), Fitzpatrick-Simmons examines both Irish and American

landscapes through a tight and consistent lyric form and voice and succeeds, in quite magical ways, in bringing the two together:

> A Child's question—Who am I?
> A new self in the Old World; I'm changed.
> The arm of a wild Atlantic still before me.
> Does it matter which—
> Bar Harbor or the mouth of Belfast Lough?
> "Leaving America," 52

The poet Jean Valentine doesn't enter into the Irish landscape as other
poets do, or at least doesn't appear to, and she doesn't explore dislocation. In her work, Ireland is grafted to her own interiors. The landscape
of Ireland emerges only as a vague color at the edge of a world concerned
with exploring the depths of other relationships—with men and women,
mothers and fathers, children, the body, and with kindred poets like Syl-
via Plath and Osip Mandelstam. Her work recalls the work of Irish poets
such as Seamus Heaney and Thomas Kinsella, poets who have spent considerable periods of their lives in the United States without feeling the
compulsion to load their poetry with direct representations of these experiences. To get at the heart of experience, Valentine frequently blocks out
the location to be better able to describe human dramas in isolation. Of
course, the west of Ireland, where Valentine lived for much of the year, is
so extraordinarily powerful in its own right that if it becomes a presence
in a poem, it may distract the reader from the soul of the poem. Yet if one
listens to Valentine's language as one listens to Beckett's, one cannot but
help hear the music of the Irish world—sounds coming as magically as
the sounds of the sea from a sea shell:

> The sound of their wings!
> Oars rowing, laborious, wood against wood: it was
> a continuing thought, no, it was a labor,
> how to accept your lover's love. Who could do it alone?
> Under our radiant sleep they were bearing us all night long.
> "Barrie's Dream, the Wild Geese," 97

Anne Kennedy reminds us in her remarkable poem "In the Women's Cancer Ward" of how shared suffering can break down national barriers. In
the cancer ward, she is united with the other women by an illness which
transcends origins, and she becomes the voice which expresses the hope
of all the women in the ward:

> Each evening after treatment
> I walk slowly into Rathgar
> to buy baskets full of nippled berries.

I can't get enough of them,
their ruby juice runs down my chin.

                                    55

I have provided a sampling of a body of work which is both impressive
and growing, and so in conclusion I would like to bring up some of the
issues which will arise in the future. First, and most obvious, is the fact
that this migration is the reverse of the movement of Irish poets to the
United States. Poets such as Seamus Heaney, Paul Muldoon, Eavan Boland, and many others have been accepted by the American poetry estab-
lishment and found both employment and audiences there. Of course, to
the Irish man or woman, this progress from Ireland to the United States
is a natural right-of-way which has long been forged by history and
practice.

Irish people, coming from a poorer country, have long considered it
their right to be able to go to the United States and seek to make it there.
Perhaps the journey to Ireland is not so simple for American poets who
are leaving a country with great resources to compete with Irish poets for
the mere scraps available in Ireland. Frequently, Americans abroad are
associated with the vulgar extremes of the American imagination—
Burger King, Barbie, the CIA, and so on—despite the fact that most of
them disavow such visions of America and come to Ireland to find respite
from them. There is the fear that Irish poetry will become as American-
ized as Irish fashion and Irish television, that these poets are part of an
American multinational conspiracy bent on repatriating the profits of
their endeavors at the expense of the locals. Such concerns are moot, however. Ireland has now fixed its sights firmly on the international stage and
has abandoned isolationism because it neither worked nor had any basis
in Irish history: The Irish have always been a people who have liked to
look beyond their shores.

Clearly, involvement in the world beyond Ireland has brought immense
cultural benefits to Ireland in poetry and in the other arts. It's not just a
question of desire; it is, as Richard Kearney and Victor Luftig point out,
one of need. American poets bring to Ireland, primarily, their great modern poetry, and Irish poets have been eager listeners.

One important aspect of Ireland which these migrant poets have ignored, for the most part, is urban Ireland. Like Synge and Yeats, they have
been almost exclusively concerned with exploring the natural beauties of
rural Ireland. As a result, they are open to the claim that they are indistin-
guishable from the denizens of tour buses who flock to the west of Ireland
each summer. In the future, these poets will have to explore the urban

centers more; they will find them as problematic and interesting as the cities they have left behind in the United States, and perhaps will rejoice in the ways these urban meccas compare and contrast with Boston, Detroit, New York, and Chicago. Ironically, these American poets are flocking to areas of Ireland which the Irish people have been deserting in droves for generations.

Dermot Bolger has said that many Irish writers who live outside Ireland are not exiles, but "commuters"—can this be applied to the writers under discussion here? Although the term is an attractive one, it is too limiting. For many of these writers, Ireland is but one stop on the road, thus migrant is a more appropriate term. Finally, how do we read these writers in relation to Irish America when many of them have no roots there? Clearly, it would be ridiculous to claim Wallace Stevens as an Irish American on the basis of his correspondence with Thomas McGreevy and because he wrote a few poems about Ireland. What has happened, of course, is that Irish culture has become so widely disseminated and influential in the United States, and travel has become so easy, that Americans bypass Irish America and come straight to Ireland. Similarly, many of the young Irish who go to America nowadays go straight to the Lower East Side of Manhattan and steer clear of an Irish American world they consider as having ground to a halt, wallowing in a time warp. What is important is that the nets be thrown out widely, and that these poets be allowed to negotiate as freely as possible in both America and Ireland. Definitions should be enlarged, inclusive, and allow both for fluidity and for a changed world. These migrations can only enrich the poetry of both Ireland and the United States.

Seven

Helena Mulkerns on the Lower East Side

As a writer of fiction, journalist, organizer, musician, and performer, Helena Mulkerns has been a central figure among the New Irish artists in New York since 1990. Her fiction, which has been widely published, and her journalism, which has appeared in *Hot Press, The Irish Times, Village Voice,* and other publications, provide an important chronicle of the lives and times of the New Irish. The East Village Irish Arts Scene is richer for Helena Mulkerns's vision and for the time she has given to organizing events and promoting the talents of the New Irish. Here she discusses her role in the New Irish arts scene.

Eammon Wall: *When did you come to America and why?*

Helena Mulkerns: The first time I came to America I was nineteen, on a student visa. I ended up in Texas, which is another story. I spent about three months there, and then committed the singular act of lunacy of buying a twenty-one-day Greyhound bus ticket, traveling to Los Angeles, San Francisco, and then all the way back across the United States to New York. On a Greyhound bus. I remember buying a map in San Francisco at the bus station and being quite dismayed when it kept unfolding and unfolding—that's a lot of bus travel!

I had always wanted to come back, and after a few years in Paris, my best friend at the time was coming to New York to study, and so I decided to come over as well. My plan was to travel down to South America and live there for a while too, but I ended up staying in New York. It's kind of addictive.

EW: *You didn't come directly from Ireland, but via France—so you didn't take a traditional path?*

HM: I think going to Europe was a tradition for the Irish long before going to America was, originally. So it's traditional in one way. But when I was sixteen I just wanted to get out, get away. I would have gone to the South Pole if I'd had the opportunity. As it happens, I went to Spain to teach English, which is definitely a tradition among young Irish women. My mother's sister did that in the early sixties, and I knew a lot of Irish teaching there in the late seventies and eighties. The great Irish author Kate O'Brien even wrote about that in 1936 in a wonderful book called *Mary Lavelle*. I went home to finish high school, but afterward spent a year teaching in Santander, in the north of Spain. I loved it. Then I went back to University College, Dublin, to do my B.A., but again, shortly after that I headed off to Paris. Dublin wasn't really a great place back then; it was still a backwater. You had Grafton Street and you had the punk rock scene, but there was nothing like all the great stuff that goes on now. Ireland has blossomed since then. I had decided I wanted to learn to speak French fluently as well as Spanish—and so I went to the Sorbonne and then ended up working for an American writer. I traveled around Europe as well, as far as Turkey. I think that Irish people just love to travel. You'll always have emigration, but there is a wanderlust in the Irish that will send them off around the planet whatever the economic situation is at home—I don't think that will ever disappear.

EW: *You are fluent in French and Spanish, so the U.S. is a strange place for you to be, perhaps?*

HM: The nice thing about big cities like New York, Paris, Los Angeles, London, etc., is that you get people from every part of the world in each one. I have quite a few friends from France, Spain, South America, and other places here in New York. I also work at the United Nations, where I use both my Spanish and French, and my (more limited) Portuguese. I also like to try and keep up my Irish language—there are quite a few different ways to do this. There's quite a substantial Irish-speaking community here, and I have attended the advanced classes run by Padraig O'Cearbhail when I can.

EW: *You are one of the New Irish. What does this term mean? Is it useful?*

HM: The New Irish was a term coined to describe this new wave of emigration from Ireland, which really started sometime in the early eighties and escalated into a flood tide from the middle to the end of the decade. Since the education system advanced significantly in Ireland from the sixties and seventies on, the emigrants were a more varied bunch than previous generations, I think, a lot of the time highly qualified. We are also of a generation that has grown up since Ireland joined the EEC, which has given it status as a contemporary state in Europe as opposed to what the rest of the world often considers being part of the British Isles. Importantly, we were also the generation that experienced punk and that whole musical movement where young Dublin bands started making their own music. That can't be underestimated, really. If Van Morrison started the ball rolling in the sixties, and Thin Lizzy and Horslips continued into the seventies, the punk revolution as exemplified by the Boomtown Rats, Stiff Little Fingers, the Undertones, etc., kicked us out of the show-band mentality and got us thinking. What happened was that we started realizing that Irish people could make their own art and draw from their own culture as opposed to simply importing it from England and America. During the eighties, the U2 star rose as high as you can get, pretty much, and along with them came Sinéad O'Connor, the Pogues, Enya, the Hothouse Flowers, etc., etc. More recently we've had bands like Ash, Therapy, and even Oasis—who are arguably Irish. In other fields, of course, you had Irish films winning Oscars, Irish poetry getting the Nobel prize, Irish fiction getting the Booker—I think that's very important, because this wave of New Irish is new not only in America, but in terms of Irish cultural development as well, as a direct result of that so-called renaissance. We don't want to forsake what we came from, and we can't leave our homeland forever like previous emigrants. We have a great, lively culture, and I think that we've come over here aware of that and being able to draw on it, as opposed to trying to forget our origins, or romanticize them.

With previous generations, the reality of what they left behind was so horrific and grim that they latched on to crocks of gold and shamrocks and all the rest of the sentimentalized Oirish American schlock. It was because they simply couldn't bear to remember the truth. Whereas the change in the Irish collective self-esteem allows us to accept what we are and appreciate our culture—whether it be the film *The General* winning John Boorman best director at Cannes, or whether it be Nuala O'Faoláin's *Are You Somebody*, which is hardly a traditional Irish memoir. One of the conflicts between the new and established Irish communities in the United States is that this mythical Ireland is still touted in everything from deodorant soap advertisements to coffee mugs, to the ever-offensive St. Patrick's Day greeting cards. It's made the New Irish community a very lively one, because they rebel against that, creating their own work. Thus, the new Ireland—and by extension the New Irish in America—have served to redefine the whole Irish identity, brushing away the postcolonial cobwebs.

EW: *What's the difference between the New Irish and the other Irish who have come to the United States over the years?*

HM: Because emigration skipped a couple of generations at home in the clement times of the sixties and seventies, many of us didn't have immediate family to bring us over legally, and so very often, the Irish found themselves illegal. This led to a necessary bonding among the younger Irish, the New Irish, as opposed to the established Irish Americans. The fifties generation and previous to that had emigrated into a ready-made infrastructure, like the parish communities, or the county associations, but we didn't have that. Groups like the Irish Immigration Reform Movement sprang up to lobby for the illegals, and gradually with wonderful Americans like Bruce Morrison, Howard Berman, Brian Donnelly, and others, we were able to become legal through the visa lotteries. So in way, although we were caucasian and English-speaking, we still had a hard time of it for many years. You'll see clashes between the old and the new, like, for instance, the case of the Irish Lesbian and Gay Organization versus the Ancient Order of Hibernians parade controversy, or the Gaelic Gotham issue. One very neat, classic example was the act of tearing up the Pope's photo on live TV, for which action Sinéad O'Connor literally fell from grace in the United States.

On the other hand, after fifteen years or so of being here, the younger element have also come to appreciate the power and potential of the Irish Americans and are keen to attract their attention and support the New Irish arts. As I said above, the New Irish have opened up a new view of Ireland for the Irish Americans. We're still working on that, I think, but it's produced some very interesting material, and some pretty good cross-pollenization. *Riverdance,* for example, was based on Irish dancing—the last skeleton in our cultural closet. Look how it's taken off. And yet it was two Irish Americans who worked with the Irish producers to make it happen. You'll see the same thing in traditional music: Many of the best musicians are Irish Americans, and the crossover and cooperation factor is very high between them and native-born musicians. I think there are a lot of young Irish Americans who are not quite content with the typical, old-fashioned take on their origins, and they are the ones who go to the gigs of young bands and attend readings, etc. They, in conjunction with the New Irish, will be the ones to topple the leprechaun syndrome—as far as they can in the powerful face of the St. Patrick's Day marketing. But this generation has come from an Ireland where that's no longer the case, and there is a sort of healthy reevaluation going on in terms of the Irish, the Irish Americans, and the New Irish. And they've been a great encouragement for young Irish over here.

EW: *You have lived most of the time in the East Village. What has attracted you to this part of the city?*

HM: I like it because it has that excitement of something just bubbling under the surface. It can be really grotty, and it's not elegant like the Upper West Side. Then again, it's the antithesis of the boring, conservative Upper East Side. The West Village is lovely, but very touristy. It's as if the arts scene moved east. Of course, it's moved even further East since, because a lot of the cutting-edge stuff is going on now directly across the river in Williamsburg, where the rent is cheaper, and there are lot of dock-yard loft-style spaces available. There are quite a few Irish over there at the moment doing excellent work. But the East Village is comfortable, and still very much a village. And there are a lot of Irish here, too. We've had a couple of hang-outs spring up over the last six or seven years or so that helped to create an interesting scene.

EW: *Why did the Irish scene start in the East Village? Was Sin-é important, and why?*

HM: Sin-é was a keystone in the whole Irish East Village scene, I think. There were already substantial numbers of Irish people living in the East Village area, who frequented local bars like Sophie's or Mona's, but they were bars without a specifically cultural focus. When Shane Doyle opened Sin-é in 1990, it was pretty much geared toward those maverick Irish in the area, and aimed to provide a place—at least in the beginning [early nineties] for young Irish artists, actors, writers, musicians, etc., who didn't all have a lot of money, etc., to come together and hang out, swap ideas, and just meet others like themselves. Doyle designed it after the typical coffeehouse, and in that regard was in fact ahead of his time. Nobody had heard of Starbucks back then, I can tell you! The name had a lot to do with it—being Gaelic for "That's it!" It intrigued Irish people, who knew what it meant. Later it would intrigue a lot of people, due to fierce marketing and overexposure, but initially it was a very cool little local unofficial arts club.

EW: *What was the role of Sin-é in inventing the Irish East Village scene?*

HM: At first, it was all just word of mouth. For my part, I walked in there one evening with a musician friend who'd heard that they had occasional acoustic music there some evenings. We formed a duo called Dún An Doras and sang with guitars, completely acoustic. I'm sure we weren't very good, but we had great fun, and that was the atmosphere. More and more musicians started dropping by, and it was very impromptu, genuine.

Shane was up for anything, and interested in local talent performing there. I know he used to like to hook people up. He was the person who introduced me to the photographer John Francis Bourke. At that point J. F. and I began to collaborate on a book project entitled *Tír Na n-Óg:*

The New Irish in America, 1981–91. We met a lot of people through Sin-é; we interviewed and photographed Karl Geary, for instance, as part of our pilot portfolio. He was the manager at Sin-é, and has since gone on to be an actor and co-owner of several other bars now. People like the actor Brian O'Byrne, who has reached great success as one of the leads in Martin McDonagh's *Beauty Queen of Leenane,* used to come in, as did Susan McKeown, the singer. At one point, we formed a small, unofficial networking outfit loosely entitled "The Irish Artists Network" and met a few times in Sin-é, then in Macauley's Bar. That was the kind of thing that was going on, and although the café wasn't the only place in the area where the Irish hung out, it was one of the few places you could go in and have a coffee or a drink, not be worried about being kicked out for loitering, and usually count on meeting someone you knew.

It was the type of place where you could organize literary evenings or readings. I think I did the first one: the launch of *Wildish Things,* a women's anthology from the Attic Press in Dublin. I also organized "East Coast Irish Voices," featuring local writers. And a St. Brigit's Day reading—a rather tongue-in-cheek all-female affair that was quite a hoot. Then at one point—I can't remember exact dates—myself, Deanna Kirk, Paul Hond, and Elizabeth Logun began performing every Saturday night in a rather anything-goes style venture called "The Clumsy Caberet." It used to start at midnight and go on until whenever we got tired, usually around 3 A.M. It was great. We used to combine our own regular songs with spots from invited musicians, poets, comedians, etc. Then if there was someone in the audience who could do a party piece, we'd have them up too. It was like a sort of weekly mad wedding reception. Once this guy got up and played a ski—an actual snow ski, with a couple of bass strings attached, and it wasn't bad! Then we had a nurse from Cavan one night, I remember, get up on a table and sing "Lili Marlene" in German! That was a trip. We were sometimes lucky enough to get really good musicians, too, as well as many of the regulars who might be playing during the week in the café, who'd just come by for fun and to hang out.

EW: *The Sin-é didn't last. Can you describe its demise?*

HM: One of the problems was that it got too popular for its own good. It was written up in every magazine from here to Tokyo, and the marketing aspect got quite good: special T-shirts, etc. I remember one day close to the "New Music Seminar" Shane asked me for advice on how to get some music industry people down, since by then he had music going every night. I was writing a lot at the time for *Hot Press,* and so had all the industry addresses, record companies, etc. I opened my filofax to him, and made a few suggestions, and while the scene that transpired around the seminar [where Irish bands were sponsored to come over by the Irish Trade Board, for three years running] was great fun, it changed Sin-é into more of an industry showcase venue, and it had become so trendy that none of the old regulars could fit in the door! When Sinéad O'Connor and U2 and the Black Crowes, etc., started dropping by, that was all written up, and instead of a local, unofficial arts center, you had a nightspot where people were practically lining up outside to get in. That was all very well and good for Shane and indeed the street-cred of the New Irish community generally, but eventually the young Irish crowd got sick of it and moved elsewhere.

EW: *Have other venues opened up to replace it?*

HM: There have been many venues, all around New York, that have catered to the New Irish community. For example, Tramps, opened by Terry Dunne in the early seventies, was an incredible blues club. Terry was also almost single-handedly responsible for the popularity of zydeco music from New Orleans in New York. He's a great guy and a fantastic musical connoisseur. When the Irish community started building up, he opened the doors of Tramps to them. A lot of bands have played there, from Gavin Friday to the Saw Doctors. Then you have Paddy Reilly's, on Twenty-eighth Street, where Black 47 originated. They became a catalyst for the kind of crossover music I was talking about, where Irish and Irish American musicians would play together. For example, the "Paddy a Go-Go" on Tuesday evenings, or Rogue's March, who do a sort of Celtic grunge. In the Bronx, you have An Béal Bocht, which catered to the community there. Likewise, the Irish Bronx Theatre Company and Macalla Theatre Company came out of the Bronx, and the scene up there has been very lively. Anseo, the low-key venue that Shane Doyle started not far from Sin-é, hosted the first performances of Tony Kavanagh's play, *The Drum,* starring Brian O'Byrne. The Scratcher, a bar on Fifth Street opened by Karl Geary, Tony Caffery, and Dermot Burke [also the owner of An Béal Bocht], launched *Here's Me Bus,* which was a popular literary quarterly founded by journalists Colin Lacey and Martin Mahoney.

You have the same kind of thing happening in other cities, too—Philadelphia, Boston, Chicago, San Francisco, New Orleans, and Los Angeles. The television series *Stateside* researched this, and provided an excellent record of how varied and active the various New Irish communities are around the United States. Boston, San Francisco, Philadelphia, and Los Angeles all have annual cultural festivals that differ from the old Irish fairs, because they provide a healthy range of young artists and musicians both from the community here and from Ireland. That's the beauty of it—

most of these events don't restrict themselves to one or the other, but try to provide a combination of native Irish and Irish American talent.

One of the more interesting aspects of this kind of fusion is what's happening on the Internet. That's like a forum for Irish culture with literally no boundaries. You can hop onto the superhighway and find out what's happening in your local town back home, or stop in at an Irish language chat room to speak Gaelic. About eleven years ago, Galway man Liam Ferrie and his wife started up an Internet newsletter called *The Irish Emigrant,* which was transmitted to thousands of young Irish around the world. It keeps people abreast of developments and news at home and has since expanded to include job listings and book reviews. Mary Robinson visited their offices on their tenth anniversary to commend them on their innovation. I currently belong to a collective of Irish women writers and artists who manifest on the web as "Banshee." It's a great opportunity.

EW: *Let's talk about your writing. How important for your writing is being in New York or America?*

HM: I don't know how important America is, specifically, to my writing. My writing includes material based in Paris, Spain, London, and other places as well. I suppose I have just spent more time proportionately of my adult life here, so it must influence me. I like the idea of Irish people living elsewhere, no matter where, and I have tried to vary my writing in this regard. The idea of moving yourself out of one culture and into another interests me. You have no essential ties to the new culture, and yet it will of course influence you. How do you reconcile the idea of home after you've been living abroad for fifteen years? How do you deal with missing out on what would normally be the security of place—in other words, family, friends, etc.? Does the new world simply replace your old one, or how much regret is there? What tools do you call upon to adapt? How much do you ever wonder what would have happened if you stayed? Of course, many Irish people are going home now, which might be the next great New Irish story.

EW: *One of your most powerful stories deals with the famine. Is the story connected to emigration, at least under the surface as a fable, perhaps?*

HM: The story "Famine Fever" was in fact inspired by a dream, where I did have a very intense vision of being in a small boat or curragh with someone who was sick, and leaving a dark coastline along with many other boats, with the sense that something terrible was being left behind. When I woke up, I wrote it down, and later the sense I made out of it was that story. People have said it's a very grim story, but it goes back to what I said about the mythology of Ireland. The idea that we are a jovial, pleasant race dancing at crossroads and tipping our caps to landlords is a mistake. We have a pretty grim heritage, we are a pretty angry people, and it's only now, after the revisionism of the sixties and seventies, when famine was a very dirty word, that we have been able to turn around and look at our history in a different light. This is also being dealt with in Irish America, too, with Famine Forums and books like *The Hungry Earth* by Seán Kenny. Some choose to still deal with it in the manner of the polite school of Irish history, as Professor Denis Donoghue once put it. A good example of this would be the recent PBS television series *The Irish in America* which made [the British politician] Trevelyan out to be a sensitive, but misunderstood chap, instead of the racist monster he really was. But it's that old joke—don't talk about the war. People are loath to reexamine history when it is ghastly, and we are only beginning to acknowledge the damage done by the famine now. The emigration after the famine was unprecedented, and you could argue that the leaving process which began then never stopped until possibly, *possibly* quite recently with all this "Celtic Tiger" business. Now there seems actually to be something to go home to, but only as a result of this huge metamorphosis that Ireland has experienced in the past ten years. A good example of this is the amount of people who turned out at the polls for the referendum recently. Whatever way you voted, it was the strongest turnout in years: For the two previous decades Southern Ireland didn't really give a damn about Northern Ireland. I think that only as a result of recent happenings, and a new, more honest evaluation of our history, are we beginning to change.

EW: *How are writers like you—New Irish living in the U.S.—viewed in Ireland?*

HM: To a certain degree, there is still a sense of isolation, since we are regarded at home as those who left. We are a new breed over here, and yet at home, the preferred image of us (although I think it is changing) is that of tragic, tears-in-our-beers emigrant, struggling as laborers, nannies, and embittered bartenders. It's not hard for those at home to feel that we've somehow *lost our claim* to Irishness, because we left. Being considered insignificant and lumped in with Irish people's limited understanding of the clichéd Irish American culture is our punishment! A lot of attention has been paid in recent years to the young writers living in London, but hopefully that interest will extend to those living over here. Colum McCann is a good example of someone who has been successful in both places.

EW: *How do you see yourself as a woman and writer—as Irish, Irish American, American? Or do these things not matter so much these days?*

HM: I don't think these things matter so much these days. The fact that I've been living here for ten years doesn't necessarily mean I get to call myself Irish American. I think that Irish people, while they can sometimes be a very inflexible bunch when they get their heels stuck in, are also some of the most adaptable, open-minded people I know. That's why you'll find them all around the world, in China or Spain or Tokyo, adapting happily to their respective new cultures, enjoying the differences, etc. The problem is that we tend to want to categorize, but I think that the diversity you see in contemporary writing is one of its most fascinating aspects. Colm Tóibín's last book, for example, dealt with a young man living in Argentina. Emer Martin's *Breakfast in Babylon* follows a young Irish woman around Europe, America, and the Middle East. Other writers, like, say, Robert McLiam Wilson with *Ripley Bogle* or Michael Collins's *The Meat Eaters* set their scenes elsewhere, but deal essentially with Irish themes. Ideally, we shouldn't have to worry about that, only about the quality of the work.

EW: *You are currently involved in* Banshee. *Can you tell me about it?*

HM: Myself and Emer Martin came up with the idea for *Banshee* because we were discussing the possiblities of getting some kind of literary venture going. It's very difficult and time-consuming to start up a magazine or a quarterly, and of course, fiction doesn't really lend itself to group effort, as such; it's something you do by yourself. We thought that a web site would be an ideal forum to get some people together and pool our resources. That way we could invite several people to contribute, in their various fields, and each have a space on the web for our own work. Collectively, we could use the site as a tool to get our work out there, and as a matter of fact, it's been going very well. We've got quite a lot of attention, and in addition to the Internet presence, we have discovered that we go down well in our live manifestation too.

We launched *Banshee* on 31 October 1997, which, of course, is the autumn pagan feast of *Samhain,* or Celtic New Year. We chose the name because we wanted something strong, loud, female, and Irish. "Banshee" seemed to fit the requirements. Our first reading, which was to launch the web site, took place in the Pink Pony Theater in Max Fish, a great, quirky Lower East Side bar. Since then, we've done a winter solstice reading (Christmas), an Imbolg reading (St. Brigit's Day/spring), a Bealtaine reading (May Day/summer), and our next Celtic date will be in San Francisco, at the Guinness Fleadh, for the summer solstice. After that there's Lughnasa, on August 1—and then our first anniversary!

We decided on a women's group simply because it is easier, and to be perfectly honest, there are enough "boy's clubs." You'd be surprised at how many men keep telling us that we need one of them to "manage" us, or to "develop our website," when we have a perfectly brilliant Irish woman, Fiona Dunne, who takes care of our site for us, without any help from the "stronger" sex! We stick pretty much to that criterion, and it seems to suit everybody. We are: writer Emer Martin, myself, poet Imelda O'Reilly, classical singer Caitríona O'Leary, actress/comedienne Elizabeth Whyte, writer and actress Jenny Conroy, writer and website designer Fiona Dunne, and our latest Banshee, a dancer named Darrah Carr, who performs both modern and Irish dance. So it's a pretty varied bunch.

So far we've played venues like Max Fish, the Knitting Factory, and Fez. We try to steer clear of typically Irish venues, because we feel that we'd rather reach out to a different audience, although having said that, we do have a large Irish following. We each have our own projects going on an individual basis, but the website and live readings help us to get that material out there, and so far it's working quite well. We've just been featured in the *Village Voice* newspaper, and Laura Metzger, a young filmmaker, is making a documentary about us. We're excited about that.

EW: *What are your current projects?*

HM: Right now I'm working on a piece for a nonfiction book which is coming out next year, entitled *Motherland*. It's basically a study of mothers and daughters, with mothers writing about daughters and vice-versa. The editor, Caledonia Kearns, has also excerpted sections from the writings of famous Irish American women, or mother figures, such as Mother Jones, Margaret Sanger, etc., in addition to gathering original material. I have interviewed my own mother, Helen, as an example of a mother and daughter parted by the emigration process. It's also a study of the generational process, how her world has differed from mine. I think it should be a very interesting book. On the other hand I have a longer fiction project that will continue as soon as I have the *Motherland* chapter finished.

Eight

Irish Voices, American Writing, and Green Cards

> In school that first year, I learned two things that began to give me some sense of self. One, I was Irish. At school, kids kept asking: What are you? I thought I was American, but in those days in Brooklyn, when you were asked what you were, you answered with a nationality other than your own. Since my parents were from Ireland, I was from a group called *Irish*.
> —Pete Hamill, *A Drinking Life*

In elementary school, as this quotation makes clear, Pete Hamill discovered who he was in the eyes of that world located beyond the family apartment: He learned that he was not just one of the Hamills of Brooklyn, or simply an American, but that he was *Irish*. I made a similar discovery in New York in the 1980s when I entered the Immigration and Naturalization Service offices, housed in Federal Plaza in downtown Manhattan, to hand in the documents which are needed when applying for a green card. Of course, I'd grown up in Ireland and carried an Irish passport; however, after a day spent in the INS offices, I began the process of learning what it means to be Irish and of trying to locate myself within the great multicultural experiment we call the United States. At the end of the day I was no longer a mere foreign graduate student or cultural tourist, but I wasn't an American either. I was somebody in between. Also that day, I recalled the coffin ships which had ferried the starving from Ireland during the potato famine—men and women who were looking back at the Irish coast for the last time as their ships made their inexorable progress away from Cobh harbor. In the United States, there lived millions of people who traced their origins to those starving souls, and it occurred to me that these far-flung souls of Irish emigration and I had much in common. I was starting to take note of my own place within the Irish diaspora. By that stage, I had been here for three years, but didn't consider myself an immigrant. I was a devil-may-care type of guy who was having a great time exploring America, that faraway country I'd grown up on which had been revealed to me in books and comics, on the screen at the Astor Cin-

69

ema, and on vinyl. Of course, you couldn't blame me for not knowing the real America—I was living in Ireland and America was an escape.

With all my documents in place, and after being fingerprinted, I rode the Federal Plaza elevator upstairs with the facts of my life gathered rather shamefully in my hands. I had arrived at heaven's gate and knew that St. Peter, or his deputy, would soon appear to pass judgment on me. Catholic judgment day has never bothered me that much; because God knows everything anyway, judgment day is in effect a show trial of the type they used to put on in the Soviet Union when Stalin was alive. But a federal judgment day is a more serious business. If I failed, I'd be booted out of the United States and separated from my wife and children.

Because so many people showed up each day to turn in papers, which was the first step toward (hopefully) obtaining a green card, I faced an interminable wait before being called up to the glass window to face an official. I looked around the vast waiting room, listening carefully. Present were people from all over the world. From eavesdropping and peeking over shoulders, I became aware of Israelis, Peruvians, Chinese, Poles, and Germans in the few rows that bordered mine, and I also became aware of people of all ages, from the young babies to the grandparents who were helping their parents take care of them. The whole world had been gathered here in front of me and the bulletproof windows, which gave the whole space an eerie and confining feeling. "There is a Berlin Wall to climb here," a young man from England told me as he nodded toward the front of the room, but I didn't agree. While he was thinking of walls, I was imagining rivers. Around me the faces of the pilgrims told stories of failures and successes, of journeys and redemptions. People had risked lives and limbs, and surrendered dignity and pride to make it to this room. Some, like the thousands who died of disease in the holds of the ships which had sailed from Ireland between 1845 and 1849, had not made it this far. I thought of the recent killings in El Salvador.

On this day, I was completing the ritual of leaving Ireland: After getting a green card, I'd have the papers to prove that I was an Irishman who'd committed myself to America. At the same time, I understood that by becoming an immigrant I was joining a larger movement of people, one which was not exclusively Irish. I learned that I shared a common bond— excitement mixed with loss—with all the other people living in America but born outside its borders. We know that no American-born person ever has to go through this process of proving her- or himself worthy in this way; we are bonded by our shared journey toward the glass window which determines so much. We have gathered our papers. Here we were, "the huddled masses." When I needed to stretch my legs, I walked toward the rear of the building. I looked out a window and saw in the distance in New York Harbor the outstretched arm and torch of the Statue of Liberty welcoming all immigrants to America. At that time the statue was covered in scaffolding as it was being spruced-up by French workmen for the celebration of its centenary. An article in the *New York Times* had said that the crew didn't want to go back to France when the job was completed, which I thought beautiful. In contrast to the fear and anxiety bred by the green card process, Lady Liberty radiated a divine and kindly warmth as she presided over the waters that had brought millions to America. The Atlantic Ocean joins Ireland to America, but it also divides the two. I admired then, and will forever, the idealism the statue signifies. The view of her in front of me and my presence there that morning in the INS offices, a postmodern Ellis Island, and the heavy symbolism of it all, overwhelmed me. Being an Irish exile is a heavy business because it's so tied up with mythology, pain, and history. When I left Ireland, I thought I was getting away from history; little did I know that I was walking right into the middle of a historical web from which there would be no escape.

In the old days in Ireland, before the advent of air travel, on the night before a son or daughter left for America a large party was held in his or her parents' house. All the neighbors were invited, there was plenty of food and drink provided, and there was music and dancing until dawn. These occasions were called "American wakes." Octavio Paz has called exile death, and "American wakes" mourned the son or daughter who, in going to America, would never be seen again, as if they had died. That morning in Federal Plaza I felt some small part of me was dying, being lost, evaporating; it was hard to explain. And I felt my love of the novelty of America wear off and be replaced by a stunned ambivalence.

Growing up in Enniscorthy, a town of about 7,000 in the southeast of Ireland, I gave no thought to the idea of nationality. I'm convinced that the Irish have always had a much more strongly defined sense of family and immediate locality than they have had of nationality and nation. Before the Norman Invasion in 1169 and the later more extensive invasions and plantations carried out by the Tudors and Stuarts in the sixteenth and seventeenth centuries, Irish society was divided up into clans ruled by chieftains. Each clan controlled a defined area which approximates the current Irish counties—the O'Neills ruled Tyrone, for example. For all intents and purposes, the land ruled by the chieftain was a country, and the idea of Ireland as a country, in the modern sense, didn't really exist, except in abstract geographical terms. The loyalties which people felt were local: to the local leader, to local topography, history, and culture. What the clans shared was a common language—Irish. It was the invaders from the outside who provided the people who lived in Ireland with the sense of being Irish. To the English, the people who lived in Ireland were Irish simply because they were not English.

To survive intact as a people, the men and women who lived in Ireland accepted their Irishness or otherness and turned this into a tool used to defend themselves. Of course, as Kerby Miller and Paul Wagner point out in *Out of Ireland,* the Irish who came to America after the famine were forced to face prejudice from an American elite who modeled themselves on their own English ancestors:

> Irish immigrants experienced [bad] treatment and prejudice from native-born Americans only in part because they were impoverished, un-skilled foreigners. They were hated because they were Irish and because they were Catholic.
>
> Most Americans prided themselves on both their British ancestry and their Protestantism. They also believed that Irish poverty was a sign of laziness and immorality, of ignorance and superstition—traits they considered inseparable from Irishness and Catholicism. (54)

Although Irish people today proudly assert their nationality, I still believe that their primary loyalties are to family and place, and that nationality comes next. For me as a child, loyalty meant pride in my home county, Wexford. Nationalism, which was learned at school, had little bearing on ordinary life. Ireland was a fact; however, Enniscorthy and County Wexford were living, breathing presences which could not be ignored. Pete Hamill's comments on his own complex sense of belonging confirm this hypothesis and show us that these predispositions have in no way been diluted by absence from Ireland. We can say, therefore, that although people living in Ireland do not live the same sorts of lives as those who live in the United States, they respond to the world in similar ways and have produced bodies of literature that have much in common. Most important of all is the fact that Irish culture has remained intact.

Under pressure in the INS offices that morning, alarm bells went off: For the first time in my life, I began to feel utterly Irish. Ironically, this declaration of nationality began at a moment when I was beginning the process of surrendering that same nationality. If I wished to define myself in the future, I would have to begin with two huge words: Irish and American. But over the years, I have revered both terms while at the same time seeking to understand them better. But the two can never be separated. I have double vision; I am doubled in every way.

Adaptability has been the key to survival for the Irish, and the written word has been vital in this struggle in Ireland and in the United States. Books have helped me locate myself. Tip O'Neill said that "all politics is local." For Irish Americans most writing is local also. *Ulysses* is, arguably, the greatest novel written this century and an enormous local book. Joyce was Irish, but he was first and foremost a Dubliner. In keeping with the narrow but rich focus of the Irish American worldview, the great concerns of Irish American writers are also local, and the writers can be best understood more in relation to boroughs or cities than in relation to nations. James T. Farrell is a Chicago writer, Pete Hamill a Brooklyn writer, Michael Stephens and Thomas McGonigle are Brooklyn and Long Island writers, William Kennedy is an Albany writer, Maureen Howard is a Bridgeport writer, and Mary Gordon and Elizabeth Cullinan are New York writers. Kennedy has said of Albany, "I don't feel I own those Irish places, but I do own Albany. It's mine" (Fanning, 352).

Like writers in Ireland, Irish American writers have had to invent a language of their own to give voice to their ethnic group. The English language that is spoken in Ireland, and which has been imported into the United States, is formed from a combination of Irish and English. In *A Portrait of the Artist*, Stephen Dedalus explains the differences between the two varieties of the same language to the English-born Dean:

> —To return to the lamp, he said, the feeding of it is also a nice problem. You must choose the pure oil and you must be careful when you pour it in not to overflow it, not to pour in more than the funnel can hold.
> —What funnel? asked Stephen.
> —The funnel through which you pour the oil into your lamp.
> —That? said Stephen. Is that called a funnel? Is it not a tundish?
> —What is a tundish?
> —That. The . . . the funnel.
> —Is that called a tundish in Ireland? asked the dean. I never heard the word in my life.
> —It is called a tundish in Lower Drumcondra, said Stephen laughing, where they speak the best English.
> —A Tundish, said the dean reflectively. That is a most interesting word. I must look that word up. Upon my word I must. (188)

One can argue that modern Irish and Irish American writing begins with Joyce, and that the familiar funnel/tundish dispute is the best explanation we have for why the writing developed as it did and emerged in the voice that it did. For Irish Catholics in Ireland, before independence and partition, to write and speak the "King's English" was impossible. To speak in that way indicated assenting to the right of the English to rule Ireland. To write down the speech patterns of the Irish in "proper English" would have been dishonest; no one spoke that way. But speaking in Irish, the mother tongue, was also difficult as over the centuries of oppression it had come to signify poverty, ignorance, and downward mobility, leading to hunger. This final point is a good measure of the degree to which the Irish were humiliated by centuries of colonization. The Irish lost their language, but couldn't speak the English of England, so they invented a hybrid. If Joyce didn't make the enterprise respectable in all reader's eyes, everyone had to admit that he made it work. He had the talent, the imagination, and the courage. He was a genius who gave the Irish a language.

The Irish brought at least two languages with them to the United States. Many of the immigrants who came here before and after the famine could not speak English, and those who did speak spoke Hiberno-English. Hiberno-English, with its hot new American flashes, quickly asserts itself in Irish American fiction in the work of the great Chicago writer Finley Peter Dunne:

> "Thrue f'r ye," said Mr. Dooley, "yet 'tis sthrange how we saw our throubles into reg'lar lenths. We're all like me frind O'Brien that had a conthract on th' dhrainage canal. He thought he was biddin' on soft mud, but he sthruck nawthin' but th' dhrift. But he kept pluggin' away." (Fanning, 237)

In both Dunne's work (the Irish American pioneer) and in Joyce's (the Irish pioneer), the language describes its speakers. When a people possess a language of their own, they will begin to assemble a literature. The Irish lost their language, but they molded English into a hybrid tongue, which they now own. Or to put it in more romantic terms: After losing one mother tongue, the Irish salvaged another from the wreck. Adaptability insures survival and guarantees a future. In both countries the fact that writers have adopted and adapted another language has distinguished them. They have emerged from a countertradition, one which historically has operated in opposition to the standard, whether British or WASP, and this has resulted in innovative and combative writing. Marginalized people usually do not write like those who marginalize them. The Irish have been smart enough to learn from the canon, but have shown scant respect for the culture which promoted it. Irish writing, both here and in Ireland, is often a kind of rocket fired over the canon's bows. In an essay on Joyce, Michael Stephens, one of Irish America's strongest voices, puts this process into perspective:

> Even being American, and raised more in the ways of American culture, the residues of that Irish past seem to imbue one's life and writings, and there is still an attitude, cultivated, no doubt, from those early myths of James Joyce, that suggests that English is a foreign language, and that coming from an Irish background one has an obligation to use this language in two ways. The first is to write it better than any native speaker—

which could as easily be construed as Polish and Conradian as Irish and Joycean—and, second, to subvert that language at every chance, knowing that the tradition you have inherited is one of experimentation. The tradition is to be original, un-English, and never bend in the pursuit of those ideals, no matter how impossible they may seem, and probably are. I still blame James Joyce for instilling these attitudes in us. (*Green Dreams,* 77–78)

It is frequently argued that Irish American writing can be easily identified by theme and point of view. Take, for example, Ron Ebest's review in a recent issue of *Éire-Ireland* of *The Next Parish Over: A Collection of Irish-American Writing,* in which he notes the overwhelming presence in the anthology of writing which is "drenched in blood and whiskey," and in which he takes the editor to task for her characterization of Irish Americans as people "bonded to our fellows by politics, by the church, by the military or the police force, by alcohol, and by a 'strange necessary suffocation of family.'" He is also unhappy with the impression given by the anthology that "relentless self-hate [is] the dominant condition of Irish-American life" (180–82). It would probably be of no comfort to Ebest to discover that similar themes are present in the works of some of their Irish contemporaries. John McGahern's fiction, considered by many to be Ireland's best, would not be out of place in this anthology. But we should not become prisoners of theme. Let's remember language. When I read William Kennedy's work out loud, I hear the language I heard in Ireland as a child. There is only a slight dilution. Charles Fanning has pointed out that Kennedy, like James T. Farrell before him, succeeds in rendering "the thoughts of an inarticulate people" (346–57). But it is a fact that much Irish American writing focuses on the downside of the culture and that some of the representations of that world are so bleak as to appear unreal. As in all literatures, however, many voices are evident, and struggles for identity are captured through a variety of lenses.

Will Irish American writing survive? Many commentators have noted that the move away from the city neighborhoods to the suburbs represents the end of the line for the Irish as a distinct ethnic group. The great historian Lawrence J. McCaffrey believes that the Irish have assimilated: They have become better educated, secured comfortable standards of living, and bought houses in the suburbs where they look and act like everyone else. The Catholic Church, parish hall, and the Democratic Party no longer play central roles in their lives. Their old apartments in the city have been taken over by new arrivals from Korea and the Dominican Republic. Their immigrant energy has evaporated. Moving to suburbia, away from the tightly knit world of city block and neighborhood, involves buying into the suburban ethos, and leads to assimilation.

Of course, when an immigrant family is able to buy a house in suburbia, it means that they have "made it" in America. Who wants to complain about this kind of success, since we all know that failure and poverty are more palatable on the page than in real life? In general, people have believed that with the election of JFK the Irish became part of the mainstream. But suburbanization has not killed Irish American writing because not every Irish American has made it there, and because these suburbs have produced some outstanding Irish American writers. Irish American writing has continued to focus on the old themes and its voice has not died. Some of the best novels, ironically or not, detail the difficulty Irish Americans face in adapting to suburbia; Thomas McGonigle's *Going to Patchogue* is a classic of this kind.

The most important contributors to contemporary Irish American poetry are James Liddy and John Montague. Liddy was born in Ireland to an American mother and has made his home in Milwaukee since the 1970s. Montague was born in Brooklyn and raised in Northern Ireland, and has made America a central concern in his poetry. The work of both poets exhibits strong American influences. Liddy initially touched down in San Francisco during the 1960s and quickly came under the influence of poets such as Jack Spicer, Robert Duncan, and the Beats. Montague crossed paths with William Carlos Williams, Robert Lowell, and John Berryman, whose work indelibly affected his own. Both Liddy and Montague have recently published volumes of collected poems.

Sense of place is a dominant characteristic of Irish poetry, and this is certainly the case in Liddy's work. In addition to exploring Irish place, Liddy has made Milwaukee, particularly its East Side, a central presence in his work of the past twenty years. What is important, though, has been Liddy's reluctance to explore Irish America and the parallel theme of exile. Instead, he celebrates the Irish past and American present and glories in the everyday as his mentors, Joyce and Kavanagh, did before him:

> Mary, Mother of Acadians,
> who makes contrary the wandering
> waters the feet of Louisiana,
> I remember your month of May
> away from pining Mother in the
> armchair, the sun outside her window.
> "The Quarter," 315

And he celebrates the freedom that being away from Ireland brings. In his explorations of Milwaukee, Liddy is drawn toward a variety of ethnic worlds—Polish, Slovenian, German—with all the circles meeting at two points, church and bar, in a poetry forever loaded with possibility:

> We scatter in booths
> longing for mattresses
> the wrong one
> sits beside us
> the cute one distant.
> Imported beers pre-mattress-music.
>   "Evening at Axel's," 325

John Montague is best known for *The Rough Field,* a poetic sequence which explores the troubled history of Northern Ireland, and for his love poetry. Less well-known, but equally important, are his treatments of Irish America. In *The Dead Kingdom,* Montague examines the lives of his distressed, exiled parents in Brooklyn:

> Christmas in Brooklyn,
> the old El flashes by.
> A man plods along pulling
> his three sons on a sleigh;
> soon his whole family
> will vanish away.
>
> My long lost father
> trudging home through
> this strange, cold city,
> its whirling snows,
> unemployed and angry
> living off charity.
>
> Finding a home only
> in brother John's speakeasy.
>   "A Christmas Card," 168

As a child Montague was sent to Ireland to be raised by his mother's family; his experience of exile was second-hand but devastating. He returned to America as a graduate student, absorbed himself in American poetry, and then, ironically, felt first-hand the sense of loss and desolation famine immigrants experienced:

> And given away to be fostered
> wherever charity could afford.
> I came back, lichened with sores,
> from the care of still poorer
> immigrants, new washed from the hold.
>   *Collected Poems,* "A Flowering Absence," 180

Montague's voice is an important one, not just for the quality of his work, but also because it shows the extent to which modern Irish men and women, for all their sophistication and education, are subject to ancient feelings of separation from Ireland.

Two important poets who emerged in 1970s are Michael Lally and Terence Winch. Lally is unashamedly Irish American, as is clear from his "South Orange Sonnets":

> When my mother died two Irish great aunts
> came over from New York. The brassy one
> wore her hat tilted and always sat with
> her legs wide apart. At the wake she told
> me loud You look like your grandfather
> the cop if you ever get like him shoot
> yourself. . . .
>
> *Catch My Breath,* 46

But in common with other younger Irish Americans, he was attracted to the fringes of American culture where in jazz and rock, and in the poets of the East and West Villages, he found kindred spirits and throbbing energies. Lally's best work, such as "My Life" in *Hollywood Magic,* is direct and subversive. In Terence Winch's work, his twin passions, writing and music, are brought together. *Irish Musicians* is an early collection of poems which focuses on the performances and lives of traditional Irish musicians in New York as they travel and play from the Bronx to the Rockaways to the Catskills. These informal sessions, or *seisúns,* are an integral part of Irish and Irish American cultural experience which have never before been written about with such feeling:

> I wish I could remember the names
> of those two old guys I used to see
> when I was a kid and spent my summers
> in Rockaway which was known as The Irish Riviera
> one of them played the fiddle the other played
> the accordion and I think one of them wore
> a top hat they just wandered in and out of bars
> playing for drinks they were just like bums
> but I still remember how fine they sounded.
>
> "The Irish Riviera," in *Irish Musicians,* 21

Winch describes these musicians as they play; he is more interested in the players themselves than in making some broad cultural statement about Irish music, which is what most writers like to do, and which frequently spoils their poetry. Winch gives these musicians their own voices. Winch is also the leader of the Celtic Thunder, a well-known Celtic band.

Kevin T. McEneaney ran Facsimile Books in New York City for a number of years before settling in upstate New York. Although of the same generation as Lally and Winch, his work is not like theirs. His recent book, *The Enclosed Garden*, finds him exploring the joys of rural and domestic life to great effect:

> The earth is plowed,
> its secret plundered,
> worms uprooted
> and bleeding in air.
> "Sowing," 37

Another factor which indicates that Irish American culture will survive has been the arrival in the United States in the last decade of a new generation of writers. The coming of prosperity to Ireland in the 1960s had reversed Irish emigration and reduced the flow of Irish coming to America to a trickle. However, with the economic downturn in the 1980s, many young Irish came to America, and many of these have begun to make their mark on both Irish and Irish American writing. The main figures in this new wave are the poets Nuala Archer, Greg Delanty, Gerard Donovan, and Sara Berkeley and the fiction writers Michael Collins, Emer Martin, Colum McCann, and Helena Mulkerns. These young voices have much in common with their Irish American contemporaries and will be important in the long run. Theirs is a double vision—Irish and American, local and international. They are the inheritors of a rich tradition and a living, breathing, screaming language.

Irish American fiction is better known than poetry. In the modern and contemporary periods certain works stand out. *Studs Lonigan* by James T. Farrell was originally published in the 1930s and is an epic account of a young man's growth to manhood in Chicago during the Depression. Like the work of Steinbeck, Farrell's work is magnificent and underrated. Mary Gordon is a controversial author, as many feel her work is too full of unrestrained rage against her upbringing, but I suspect that the criticism is unjustified. Instead, I would argue that she writes with anger and passion about the difficulty women have experienced growing up in strict, Catholic households in a patriarchal society. Her protagonists, to paraphrase Joyce, are trying to flee from the nightmare of history. William Kennedy's Albany novels are justly famous and he has never written a bad book; *Billy Phelan's Greatest Game* and *Ironweed* are classics. Like Thomas McGonigle, Michael Stephens grew up on Long Island. Stephens published two great books in 1994: a novel, *The Brooklyn Book of the Dead*, and a collection of essays, *Green Dreams: Essays under the Influence of the Irish.*

Another notable collection by an Irish American poet is Nuala Archer's *The Hour of Pan/amá*. Archer was born of Irish parents in New York but spent much of her early life in Central and South America, factors which have played an important role in shaping her work. Her startling and electric images bring to mind the poetry of Lorca and the deep image poetry of Diane Wakoski:

> The same slit that zips the Pacific Ocean to the Atlantic unzips the connection between continents. The same canal that velcros, slashes. Both the Atlantic and Pacific breezes wing their salt traces through her. For her, like rain, the setting is tropical. Water is sutured, land is unstitched. It was a horrific operation. ("The Hour of Pan/amá," 3)

Sexual discovery, family, the past, and landscape are beautifully interwoven in this impressive book.

What I have provided is an incomplete personal selection to indicate one starting point for readers who wish to get involved in this rich and complex field. Others can provide more detailed beginnings. The book which best surveys the literature of Irish America is Charles Fanning's *The Irish Voice in America,* whereas the best historical overviews are Lawrence J. McCaffrey's *The Irish Diaspora in America* and Kerby Miller's *Emigrants and Exiles: Ireland and the Irish Exodus to North America.* These writers create a larger picture of the Irish pilgrims' progress.

The Irish voice remains strong in the United States. Despite moves away from the old urban repositories of culture, it survives. Just when you feel that nothing is happening, an exciting new writer emerges in whose words one again hears the ancient music. And it is wrong to think that the Irish have assimilated and are no longer an ethnic group. In fact, many writers are best read in a multicultural context. Alice Walker and Mary Gordon are not as far apart as some would have us believe, and Michael Stephens's concerns about language are similar to those voiced by Sandra Cisneros. Irish American writers describe a teeming, explosive, and varied world. This is our language. We speak it. It belongs to us. For an immigrant like me, Irish American writing is a journey into light, a journey home.

Nine

Roger Boylan in His Own Words
Q & A

Killoyle, Roger Boylan's first novel, was published by Dalkey Archive Press in 1997. It is a comic exploration of life in contemporary Ireland. Though born in the United States, Boylan was raised in Ireland, Switzerland, France, and Italy, as his family followed his father as he installed electronic carillon bells in churches throughout Europe. Like many contemporary Irish writers, Boylan is possessed of an outlook that is simultaneously local and global and that has shaped his esthetic.

Eamonn Wall: *From what I have gathered you were born in the U.S., but were raised in Ireland. Could you provide some background on this?*

Roger Boylan: I was indeed born in the U.S. but grew up in Europe, not only in Ireland (Dublin and the North) but also, because of the peripatetic aspect of my father's profession (he was a kind of journeyman electronics technician and specialized in the installation of electronic carillon bells in churches) in places like Geneva, Paris, and Rome. I went to a secular boarding school-type institution and received my higher education at the University of Ulster in Coleraine, County Derry, and Edinburgh University in Scotland.

EW: *What did you study in college—literature, languages, electronics, banking?*

RB: Pub interiors, mostly, with a little time out for Irish history at Coleraine and Romance languages and comparative religion at Edinburgh.

EW: *Other Irish writers have spent part of their childhoods in the U.S. and it has had a significant influence on what and how they have written: John Montague, Eavan Boland, Padraic Fiacc, for example. Has it been important in your life/work?*

RB: Not really. My American childhood ended at age five, when my father, then flush, sent my mother and me across the ocean aboard the liner *Queen Elizabeth.*

EW: *But you are back in the U.S. again now! I wonder whether you consider yourself an Irish writer, an Irish American writer, or whether you try avoid such designations?*

RB: My cultural heritage is European, Irish, and American, in no particular order. I suppose this makes me at least as much an American writer as, say, Nabokov. I've always thought the ideal world-citizen would be a cosmopolitan American, Judeo-Christian and Western in heritage, proud of his or her own cultural tradition but open to the best in other traditions without automatically giving any of them the benefit of the doubt.

EW: *As an Irish writer, you belong with such innovators as Aidan Higgins and John Banville. As an Irish American writer, your work has a lot in common with the work of James McCourt, Thomas McGonigle, and Michael Stephens. Do you feel you belong with either group?*

RB: That isn't for me to say, as I'm unacquainted with the work of either group, although your question certainly arouses my interest in getting to know one or two of these writers. In fact, I read little contemporary fiction.

EW: *Do you feel there's little in contemporary fiction to get excited about, or are you just too busy?*

RB: Both. I have a family and a workaday job, so I'm kept busy. Anyway, too much contemporary fiction seems to be either part of somebody's Ph.D. dissertation or TV in print form. Still, I'm sure there are diamonds in the dross. It's the enduring one percent or so of all art that you have to look for, in any age.

EW: *Your novel, as its title tells us, is "An Annotated Tale of Modern Ireland." It also seems to be an annotated tale of Irish fiction. It playfully parodies such things as the Big House novel (Spudorgan Hall) and John Banville's* Book of Evidence *(page 220) where you allude to the MacArthur and the Attorney General "affair." Can you comment on this?*

RB: There is a bit of the Big House novel there, because I've always liked the literature of the Anglo-Irish ascendancy and its descendants (Somerville and Ross, Yeats, Elizabeth Bowen, William Trevor, etc.), but I've never read Mr. Banville's work, although he sounds interesting. The Attorney General affair I was thinking of happened during the first Haughey administration, back in the early eighties, and involved far more sordid things—sex and murder among them, if memory serves—than the one alluded to in *Killoyle*.

EW: *What exactly attracts you to these Anglo-Irish writers—religion, heritage, view of Ireland, style, esthetic, or something else?*

RB: They represent the consummation of the shotgun marriage between Ireland and England. They were the descendants of aristocrats, for the most part, fallen on hard times, and uncertain where they belonged. I find this very appealing, for personal and ancestral reasons. Their search for identity was the result of divided loyalties, of course. Even many of those who stayed in Ireland after 1922 weren't quite sure of their allegiance, although some did become great patriots, as if to compensate: Yeats, Erskine Childers, Douglas Hyde. The Anglo-Irish writers combined the classical tradition of English literature with the Irish love of poetic narrative.

EW: *Contemporary Ireland, as you represent it, is in a state of near collapse?*

RB: On the contrary, it may be doing too well for its own good. What worries me on a cultural level isn't poverty and recession—Ireland's an old hand at those—but the homogenization of life, in which the suffering is more along the lines of not being able to run the Boston Marathon or not being able to afford a satellite TV dish: somewhat less extreme, in other words, than the bone-deep variety of suffering that prompts the question "What's it all about?," which is, of course, the genesis of art. The amenities of modern life, some of them wonderful, some of them not—things like affordable cars, a computer in every home, rock music everywhere, and the Internet binding us all—exact a spiritual and cultural price. Incidentally, the English language suffers, too. It's being infected by international bureaucratese, MBAspeak, the way rock lyrics swept the world in the seventies and eighties: Financial whiz kids in Dublin talk about "facilitating" and "being proactive" and "rightsizing" and so on, just like their counterparts in London, Tokyo, New York, and Austin, Texas. This is sad, because Irish English used to be just about the richest, most subtle and funniest anywhere. Maybe it still is. Maybe I'm just being sentimental.

EW: *Joyce, in* Portrait of the Artist, *explores this same idea in his debate with the dean over the tundish/funnel. Would you advocate policies similar to those put forward in France which would preserve Irish culture:*

Limit the amount of rock music allowed on the radio, keep Americaspeak out of the dictionaries, etc.?

RB: Given the essentially democratic nature of the English language and the English-speaking nations, I don't think this would work. I find it quite easy to avoid listening to rock music, and as for "Americaspeak," although I deplore the kinds of deadening infelicities I described—memospeak, actually, an international dialect—for better or for worse the English language is reaching its global zenith as *American* English: America is where the language comes from, today. The French are just reacting in their own way to lost prestige, and as much as I love their language, which I've known since childhood, theirs is a losing battle. *Le weekend, le marketing,* and *le look* represent the worst nightmare of the Académie Française, but they're the words the average French citizen uses. Fair's fair: English took from French, now French is taking from English.

EW: *Do you suspect that the world is becoming illiterate, Ireland included, and that writing is suffering and/or dying?*

RB: Well, despite the foregoing, not really. Standards are undeniably sagging, but we have the education bureaucrats to thank for that, not writers who, after all, are the ones who do the actual writing. Some of the world's greatest literature has come from almost totally illiterate times and places. What was the percentage of literate Russians when Dostoevsky was writing *The Brothers Karamazov,* or of Germans when Goethe wrote *Faust?* Not to mention the India of the Upanishads, or the Rome of Pliny. As a matter of fact, there might be a real chance of the Internet reviving the belles lettres tradition: I can imagine a modern Flaubert and Turgenev sending lengthy missives back and forth through cyberspace in a fraction of the time it took the originals to assemble pen, ink, paper, postage, etc. But that could be wishful thinking.

EW: *When did you ask yourself "What's it all about?" Is this what prompted you to be a writer?*

RB: My love of language and art, and my fascination with the everyday struggle of life, prompted me to be a writer. "What's it all about?" is the eternal question, reiterated every day. God's apparent absence (or, worse, presence) during catastrophic suffering is a colossal impediment to faith; on the other hand, the idea of a mechanistic, meaningless universe is intolerable. "In the absence of God, everything is permissible," as Ivan says to the Inquisitor in *Karamazov. That* is impermissible; so, back to the question, ad infinitum—or until faith casts aside reason and removes all doubt!

EW: *European Union and travel, represented by Emmet Power's move to Italy in your novel, have done little to improve things?*

RB: A lot, with the caveat expressed above, although I think Emmet moved because he was fed up with the goings-on at Spudorgan Hall and because he wanted to add something special to his marriage; also, he'd always wanted to go to Italy.

EW: *Are there living writers out there with whom you feel a particular kinship? Who are they and why are they important?*

RB: The writers whom I regard as inspiring combine love of language with humor and a willingness to take on the big questions (life, death, and love) without polemicizing. In Britain, Kingsley Amis and Anthony Burgess, both recently deceased, qualified eminently. Among contemporary Irish writers, Edna O'Brien, John McGahern, Brian Moore, Brian Friel, Mary Lavin, Bernard MacLaverty, Anthony Cronin, and William Trevor would all qualify too, to greater or lesser degrees. Their atmosphere, character, and style distinguish them from the run-of-the-creative-writing-mill. I also have to mention J. P. Donleavy and Benedict Kiely, both of whom I have long admired. Among continental Europeans, I think the Swiss novelist Jacques Chessex is one of the little-known great writers of our time, and I like Gregor von Rezzori, the Wandering Austrian; also Michel Tournier when he's not being too bleak, and Patrick Susskind, likewise. Not too many living Americans come to mind. Russell Banks? Updike, occasionally (good stylist), but he writes too much. I'd like to include Edward Abbey, although he died in '89: irreverent, opinionated, funny. But as I said, I read little contemporary fiction. When I have the time to read, I go back.

EW: Killoyle *reminds me of the work of Flann O'Brien in its playfulness, humor, and intricate organization. Can I safely cite him as an influence? Milo's name invites this comparison!*

RB: You score a bull's-eye here. The discovery of Flann O'Brien's work was my writer's road to Damascus. His near-insane precision of language, unremitting absurdity, mixing of the mundane and the supernatural: Didn't Joyce himself call him "a writer with the real comic spirit"? Burgess, too, was a devotee. I return to O'Brien (or O'Nolan, or Myles) whenever I can, especially *At Swim-Two-Birds* and *The Third Policeman,* but also (in deference to my publisher) *The Dalkey Archive,* and even his minor Keats and Chapman pieces cheer me up when I'm low.

EW: *And I find the influence of Beckett present also—the Beckett of* Murphy *and* Molloy. *When you were growing up were these the sort of writers which captivated you?*

RB: Yes. Actually, Beckett's been misrepresented. Like Dostoevsky, he's much funnier and more accessible than the lit-crit crowd would have us believe (they want to keep great writers to themselves, the way the Catholic Church traditionally kept the Bible away from the average churchgoing punter). There's great compassion in Beckett's work, and hilarity, and the same kind of questioning of God and the universe you find in the Russians, who were, as a matter of fact, my favorite reading when I was young, especially Dostoevsky, Gogol, and Goncharov (Tolstoy's great, but lacks humor). I believe there's a strong emotional and spiritual kinship between Celts and Slavs, and it comes out in their subversive, slightly crazy view of the world (Jaroslav Hasek's a good non-Russian example), as well as in their devotion to language. Nabokov was a fine example of this, and he's long been one of my favorites; in fact, he reminds me of Flann O'Brien. *The Gift* and *The Third Policeman* are not so far removed, thematically. As to other influences: French was my second language when I was growing up, so I got to know Rousseau and Voltaire (living in Geneva helped) pretty well; I preferred, and prefer, Voltaire. I read widely among the naturalists—Flaubert, Maupassant, Zola—and, of the moderns, Céline's *Journey to the End of Night* and Tournier's *Le Roi des Aulnes* (*The Alder King*) bowled me over. I took to the Italians Svevo (Joyce's protégé), Buzzati, and Moravia, and to the Austrians Schnitzler and Musil. Swiss literature tends to be underrated, for some reason. Ramuz, de Pourtalès, Frisch, Dürrenmatt, and Jacques Chessex all deserve top marks, in my opinon. I've also been deeply impressed by Kawabata, and Borges, and Octavio Paz, and the Portuguese poet Fernando Pessoa.

EW: *Unlike many writers nowadays, you are not part of a university. Do you think that the lit-crit crowd, as you call them, have taken the fun out of reading? What can be done about it?*

RB: Yes, I think they have taken the fun out of reading, just as their ideological forebears in the Politburo tried to take the fun out of life. Like all ideologues, they—the deconstructionists, the Lacanites, the postmodernists—fear the individual spirit, that is, art, and they condescend to those who invoke beauty. They prefer to speak of politics, and semiotics, and symbolism. It's all a mish-mash of psychoanalysis, sociology, and politics, and none of it has anything to do with literature. What can be done about it? Ignore them, if possible; oppose them, if not.

EW: *Are you a self-taught writer who picked it up? Does this type of "training" have advantages? Certainly the reading you have done is much more varied than anything a university syllabus might offer? You came to America but didn't go the creative writing program route.*

RB: Yes, I am self-taught, through reading other writers good, bad, and indifferent. I would hesitate to recommend this to anyone else; it's just the way it happened to me. It certainly isn't a shortcut to fame and fortune. On the other hand, the various syllabi of our multitudinous creative writing programs remind me of a comment of Robert Mitchum's when he was asked about the merits of the Method school of acting: "It's like trying to learn to be tall." One can be coached, certainly, but taught? I wonder.

EW: *What do you set out to achieve in your writing? What's your purpose?*

RB: That's a hard one. I'm not sure I'm consciously aware of having a purpose. I suppose I want to amuse, entertain, and move the reader, and to satisfy myself that I've presented an honest view of life. I want the respect of my peers and, maybe most of all, I want to write what I like to read.

EW: *The sense of place is very important in Irish writing. In* Killoyle, *however, you subvert this. Is this deliberate?*

RB: Yes, in homage to *Molloy* and *At Swim-Two-Birds,* in which place, time, and identity are all subverted.

EW: *The book is located somewhere in the southeast of Ireland but the exact location is impossible to identify given the contradictory clues. At times, we are in Rosslare Harbour in the hotel overlooking the ferry, but at other times we are in Waterford (perhaps). Waxford is how Donegal people pronounce Wexford! Killoyle is a composite, constructed of bits from different places, wouldn't you say?*

RB: Yes, indeed. The Irish seaside resort I know best is Portrush, County Antrim [now Coleraine District], where I spent a lot of time when young. Killoyle might be seen as a transplanted Portrush: Ulster in the southeast, with touches of Bray, County Wicklow, Ballsbridge, Dublin, and maybe the hint of Bundoran [the promenade] or Knock [the shrine]. You'd find a Donegal accent or two in a place like that, and Emmet's pure County Armagh [the pub his father owned, the Shandon Bells, is a real place in Keady].

EW: *The characters, perhaps, despite their names, are also drawn from bits and pieces of the real world of the southeast? It's all deep in lore? How did you go about writing the novel and bringing it all together?*

RB: Actually, there's probably more of the lore of the North, and Dublin, in it than genuine southeast. As for how I went about it, I wrote most of it while I was employed as a technical writer at Chase Manhattan Bank in New York. I had the good fortune to be assigned a desk in a room otherwise inhabited solely by computers whose screens it was my duty to supervise. This meant being left alone for sometimes hours at a stretch. As far as I know, the boss never caught on, although he did look in once and shout, "What the hell are you doing in there, anyway, writing a novel?" It would never have occurred to him that that was exactly what I was doing, between edits of technical data and memos. I kept in touch with the real world of Irish letters via lunchbreak and subway reading of (among others) Beckett, Flann O'Brien, Benedict Kiely, and Sean O'Faoláin. The *Irish Times* and the *Blue Guide to Ireland* helped, too, but mostly it was Mnemosyne [the goddess of memory].

EW: *Chase Manhattan unwittingly sponsored your writing and all of this culminated in your novel being written and published and Chase being acquired by Chemical! Are these events related? It's certainly a Flann O'Brien-like scenario!*

RB: The more so as the new Super Chemical Bank is actually called Chase Manhattan Bank, the name of the bank taken over. The goat swallows the python! No, there's no cosmic connection among these events that I'm aware of. By the way, a further bit of irony is that I'm now working for a publisher and have no time to write, whereas when I was working for a bank I managed to write one and a half novels.

EW: *You were writing this book during the greedy 1980s. As vast sums were being made by Ivan Boesky and Michael Milken,* Killoyle *was taking shape? Comment.*

RB: Milken and Boesky were, of course, both admired and reviled, like naughty Greek gods ("Ah, that Hermes!"). Actually, they were probably more admired than reviled, because to criticize them for making a fast couple hundred million on the side would call into question the entire ethical structure of the Wall Street arbitrageur. On that subject, I remember Black Monday, October 1987, when the Dow Jones fell 700 or more points and all the high-rolling yuppies who would normally have been plotting mergers and leverage buyouts over margaritas at the South Street Seaport were huddled after hours on the sidewalk outside the Stock Exchange, swapping rumors, trying to fend off sudden intimations of mortality. Another memorable day: As I was in my computer room, toggling furtively from the legitimate bank screen ("Projected First-Quarter Costs, Fiscal Year 1993") to my secret hideaway on the southeast coast of Ireland (a.k.a. *Killoyle*), there was a bang and the whole Chase building shook in sympathy with the World Trade Center, which had just been bombed. All these things were happening as *Killoyle* was gestating, and presidents and corporate magnates were coming and going in the busy world just outside the door of my computer ward. One day I actually rode up in the elevator with David Rockefeller. Our conversation went like this:

SELF: Good morning.

DAVE: Good morning.

This is the sum total of the Boylan–Rockefeller dialogues.

EW: *Was it difficult to write under these circumstances in this room of computers or did the notion of stealing time energize you? Were you like a child in a candy store with all the grown-ups departed?*

RB: It was a bit nerve-wracking, and having to be on the alert for prying eyes meant that narrative continuity suffered somewhat. I used to arrive about 5:45 A.M. and get in a good hour's editing of the previous day's writing before the grown-ups arrived—unless, as sometimes happened, the night shift were still on the premises, wrestling with a programming problem. However, I always had a stack of dummy memos and reports at hand, and claimed to be up against all kinds of backlogs and deadlines if anyone inquired.

EW: *Your descriptions of writing in the room and reading on the subway indicate that writing and reading are very much labors of love. Would you agree?*

RB: Absolutely. Under inimical circumstances, writing and reading become the mirror image of a secret vice: a virtue practiced in secret. They are what keep me (relatively) sane.

EW: *Have you intentionally sought to mix fact and fiction as Irish writers are wont to do? Murphy and Doreen remind me of Eddie Gallagher and Rose Dugdale, for example!*

RB: You have a point, especially with Doreen and Rose Dugdale. Rose wasn't an inspiration in my conscious mind, but in the good old subconscious, who knows?

EW: *And Milo Rogers is part of what the poet Patrick Kavanagh called the "standing army of Irish poets, 100,000 strong"?*

RB: Yes. I forgot to mention Kavanagh as an influence. I'm generally less drawn to poetry than to fiction, but I respond instantly to most of Kavanagh's work, and not just to his verse. *The Green Fool* was pretty good, too: pathetic, yet hilarious. My favorite combination.

EW: *Of course, Killoyle doesn't appear to be autobiographical, but at the same time no reader will ever believe that an Irish writer's novel is all fiction. How have you incorporated materials from your own experience into the novel?*

RB: Alas, there's more of me in Milo than either of us would care to admit. And Emmet, too. And of me, and of Portrush, in Killoyle generally.

EW: *What prompted you to forsake New York for Texas? Perhaps you got caught writing novels on company time! I'm sure that Flann O'Brien wrote most of his newspaper columns on company time too!*

RB: No, I was never caught, nor snitched on. My daughter, Maggie, had just been born, and New York, for all its greatness, isn't the best place to raise a child. Fortuitously, Liz, my wife, who is a historian, had been offered a job as assistant history professor at Southwest Texas State University here in San Marcos; we hesitated perhaps thirty seconds before deciding to make the move. We miss New York, but a small town in Texas has its advantages, like low crime and being able to afford a house with some land. By the way, not least of the advantages is being able to drive again, which you can't do in Manhattan unless you're rich. Driving is important, because cars have always been a hobby of mine.

EW: *Any plans for another novel? What are you working on now?*

RB: When time permits, I'm working on a novel provisionally titled "Gustave Adored," set in Geneva, about an alcoholic Swiss schoolteacher who starts having visions: Are they the DTs, or is he a genuine mystic? (I think the latter.) I'm also trying to peddle two other completed efforts, one a novella about Mozart, the other a comedy of manners set in a fictional city in England called St. Anselms, a kind of English Killoyle.

Ten

"*Even Better Than the Real Thing*"
Brian Moore's *The Great Victorian Collection*

That the United States and Canada figure prominently in Brian Moore's
work is hardly surprising given that he lived in one or the other of these
countries for over forty years. But Moore's novels are not merely set in
these North American nations; on the contrary, one finds in *An Answer
from Limbo, Fergus, Black Robe, Cold Heaven,* and other works detailed
examinations of many aspects of the New World experience. In fact, one
of Moore's most important contributions to Irish fiction has been his ability to forsake Ireland, the traditional stomping ground of modern Irish
writers, and report on other worlds with confidence and ease. This aspect
of Moore's work has had an enormous influence on a whole generation
of younger Irish writers such as Colm Tóibín, Emer Martin, Sebastian
Barry, and Glenn Patterson. But despite the wide range of his landscapes,
the central themes, concerns, and explorations one finds in Moore's fiction are generally part of the traditional domain of Irish fiction. Frequently, protagonists are pushed into crises as a result of unfulfilled sexual
longings or conflicts between religious rules and human desires, or between individuals and their families or societies, and woven deeply into
these fabrics one recognizes such diverse and hoary chestnuts as politics,
guilt, and miracles. However, since such obsessions are simultaneously
Irish and universal, Moore has retained a loyal and diverse audience
through nineteen novels.

Unlike his other works, *The Great Victorian Collection* (1975) is, for
the most part, as much concerned with place as with theme, and is
Moore's attempt to describe where he lived (the United States and California) to his reader. It is a book born out of the experience of absorbing
America and written with some of the same hostility which governs his
portraits of Belfast in *The Lonely Passion of Judith Hearne* and *The Feast
of Lupercal* and of Canada and Canadians in *I Am Mary Dunne.* Here,
Moore, who distributed socialist literature on Belfast street corners as a

91

young man, takes particular aim at American business, its mass media, and its university "experts" (O'Donoghue, xii). At the same time, *The Great Victorian Collection* is a very postmodern work and something of a landmark in Moore's career, one in which he puts on display all he has learned from studying the technical innovations Borges and García Márquez have introduced into fiction. The view of America in general, but of Southern California in particular, is born of Moore's belief that the absence of a sense of history has created in many Americans, as Umberto Eco has noted, "the frantic desire for the Almost Real [which has arisen] as a neurotic reaction to the vacuum of memories" (31). Such creations as the Palace of Living Arts in Los Angeles and the Hearst castle in San Simeon are "Absolute Fakes [and the] offspring of the unhappy awareness of a present without depth" (Eco, 31). Ironically, Moore's *Collection* is "real," though it is also the vehicle used to explore the strangeness of contemporary America. When I interviewed Moore in 1990, he stated:

> I was very stimulated when I first came here—by the freedom and the open society. However, the longer I've lived here the more I realize it's like Northern Ireland: it's a complicated situation. I'm not stimulated at all by where I live now [Malibu, California]. (Moore, interview by Eamonn Wall, 368)

The Great Victorian Collection is an alien's look around his adoptive state and country. Both author, protagonist, and objects are removed from their proper domains, and this is why they appear so strange and out-of-touch in California, a capital of the postmodern.

The "Great Victorian Collection" is the creation of Tony Maloney, a twenty-nine-year-old assistant professor of history at McGill University. Maloney, after attending a conference at Berkeley, drives south in a rented car and checks into the Sea Winds Motel in Carmel-by-the-Sea. That night he dreams that a vast collection of artifacts from the Victorian period has been assembled in the parking lot of the motel. When he wakes in the morning he discovers what he has been dreaming about has come to be:

> It was morning. I was in the motel room I had dreamed about, that same room in which I had gone to sleep. I got out of bed and barefoot, wearing only my pajama trousers, went to the window, raised the blind, and saw that same pink sunrise. There, below me, just as in the dream, was the large open-air market and the maze of stalls occupying the entire area of the parking lot which had been empty last evening. I opened the window, climbed down onto the main aisle, and began to walk along the aisle, exactly as I had done in my dream, coming to the selfsame crystal fountain which I recognized now as the work F & C Osler, a marvel of casting, cut-

ting, and polishing of faultless blocks of glass, erected originally in the
transept as the centerpiece of the Great Exhibition of 1851. (7–8)

Maloney has dreamed up the largest collection of Victorian artifacts in
the world. Many of the pieces are not just similar to but are identical to
pieces in English museums, while others are pieces which had been lost.
The existence of the collection is confirmed by a man out walking who
asks Maloney, "What the heck is this, some kind of exhibition? How in
God's name did they get it up so fast?" (10). The size of the collection is
revealed by the irate motel and parking lot owner, who berates Maloney:
"What's all this junk? How in hell did this stuff get in here? I don't believe
it. A fountain! I've got to be dreaming. . . . How did you get all those
structures up? You must have used fifty trucks" (11–12).

   Although Moore is often considered a traditional writer, it is clear
from *The Great Victorian Collection* and some other more recent novels
that he has been influenced by innovative novelists, and by Borges in particular. Borges's fiction often resembles books of legal evidence in which
the individual's whole life, or some part of it, is examined dispassionately.
Borges refers to his fiction as essays: Instead of providing a story, Borges
provides a gloss on the margins of a story as a substitute for a story itself.
He's a scholar of nonexistent texts. Therefore, Borges's stories approxi-
mate to Maloney's collection.

   A good example of a typical Borges fiction is "An Examination of the
Work of Herbert Quain," a short story, appropriately enough, with an
Irish setting:

> Herbert Quain has just died at Roscommon. I was not astonished to find
> that *The Times Literary Supplement* allots him scarcely half a column of
> necrological piety and not a single laudatory epithet but is corrected (or se-
> riously qualified) by an adverb. *The Spectator*, in its pertinent issue, is un-
> questionably less laconic and perhaps even more cordial, but compares
> Quain's first book, *The God and the Labyrinth*, with a work by Mrs. Aga-
> tha Christie, and others with books by Gertrude Stein: evocations which
> no one would consider inevitable and which would not have gratified the
> deceased. Quain, for that matter, was not a man who ever considered him-
> self a genius; not even on those extravagant nights of literary conversation
> on which a man who has already worn out the printing presses inevitably
> plays at being Monsieur Teste or Doctor Sam Johnson. . . . He was very
> clear-headed about the experimental nature of his books: he thought them
> admirable, perhaps, for their novelty and for a certain laconic probity, but
> not for their passion. (*Fictions*, 66)

The tone of this paragraph (cool, ironic, speculative) and the diction (specialized, to distance narrator from subject) is closer to what one might

find in a dull scholarly journal than in a work of fiction. Borges makes no attempt to convince his reader he is telling a story; no significant events are foreshadowed, and the imaginary Irish writer Herbert Quain is not made at all interesting. Borges reminds us, as does Beckett, that traditional, plot-driven storytelling is highly artificial and must be discarded. What makes the preceding paragraph, and Borges's fiction in general, so captivating is its irony and cleverness. "Necrological piety" is a beautiful send-up of the kind, but insincere words composed by obituary writers, while the coupling of Quain with Agatha Christie and Gertrude Stein is both funny and confusing. Of course, Borges makes no effort to determine which of these authors Quain is closest to. Borges and Quain may be the same person: The title of Quain's first book, *The God of the Labyrinth,* is close to the title of Borges's second, *Labyrinths.* In addition, Quain's observation, summarized by Borges's narrator, that his work is known for "its novelty and for a certain laconic probity," could also be applied to Borges's own fiction (*Fictions,* 66).

The Great Victorian Collection is also written in the form of an investigative report. Moore, like Borges, or a scholar, or a police officer, keeps his distance. Without intruding, the narrator provides the process with an area to unfold itself. The merit of Quain's work is debated by the experts who review it in journals, and, in like manner, experts are brought in to decide whether Maloney's collection is authentic. Of course, because the motives of such experts are suspect, their integrity is undermined. Unlike Borges, Moore does not abandon the traditional ways of writing novels. Instead, he retains plot, foreshadowing, and so on and adds elements which appeal to him, which he has found in his readings of the works of Borges, the Magic Realists, and such "superfiction" writers as John Barth and Robert Coover.

Why have both Borges and Moore resorted to the fantastic in much of their work? Borges explains it best in his preface to *Doctor Brodie's Report:* "I have set my stories some distance off in time and space. The imagination, in this way, can operate with greater freedom" (12). However, Borges still considers himself a realist. For the fantastic to be convincing in writing, it must be treated as if it were real so the reader will think it real. Before writing *The Great Victorian Collection,* Moore's work fit in to a traditional Irish groove: He wrote of variations on a theme of poverty—spiritual, sexual, economic, artistic. What made this early work so compelling was the quality of the writing, its honesty, and its variety of settings. Furthermore, these novels were urgent and earnest. However, in three novels—*Catholics* (1972), *The Great Victorian Collection* (1975), and *Cold Heaven* (1983)—he produced, for him, a new, more speculative, dispassionate, and more imaginative kind of fiction. Of course, because he was raised a Catholic in Ireland—the country with one of Europe's greatest treasure troves of folklore where myth and religion, past and present, fact and fiction are often inseparable—it seemed natural for Moore to combine what he had inherited from Ireland with what he had discovered in America. Furthermore, one can speculate that perhaps *The Great Victorian Collection* is, at least to a degree, a kind of ironic stock taking of Moore's own career to date and that the artifacts strewn about the California parking lot, being examined by onlookers and experts, are figures representing both Moore's novels and their readers and critics. One unavoidable conclusion, considering Maloney's fate, is that Moore believes that the creators of novels or Victorian collections play second fiddle to the image-makers, spin doctors, and moneybags who seek to profit from the creativity of others.

Why, one might ask, does Maloney have his dream in Carmel, and not in his hometown of Montreal, or in England? An obvious answer is that Carmel is close to where Moore lives; a fuller answer, however, is more complex. In an ingenious essay on the novel, Seamus Deane suggests why this novel had to be set in California:

> Brian Moore's *The Great Victorian Collection* and Umberto Eco's essay "Travels in Hyperreality" were both published in 1975. The reason for Eco's "journey into hyperreality," from the Hearst castle in San Simeon, to Lyndon Johnson's mausoleum in Texas, the now-defunct Palace of Living Arts in Los Angeles, to the California Disneyland, the Florida Disneyworld and so on, is to discover "instances where the American imagination demands the real thing and, to attain it, must fabricate the absolute fake. . . ." One point, repeatedly and ingeniously made by Eco, leads directly to Moore's novel, and it is appropriate that the J. Paul Getty Museum in Malibu, close to where Moore lives, should offer the most telling illustration of it. The Getty museum is one of the greatest of its kind. It displays works of "unquestionable authenticity." But it also contains an edifice called the Villa of the Papyruses of Herculaneum which is a reconstruction of a building which no longer exists in its entirety and is, in its totality, a supposition. It has been (re)created by experts. (74)

Ironically, Maloney's collection, since it is just like the real thing, is not a fake. The fake in this novel is "The Great Victorian Village," constructed by Management Incorporated a few miles distant from Maloney's collection, which is mixture of Las Vegas, Disneyland, and the Crystal Palace. It is, in Eco's words, a "hyperreal" place (43). The village had to be constructed because road access, parking, and space for development were lacking at the original site. Also, it was felt that a simpler collection would attract a wider audience. The flagellation chambers of the collection and other kinky areas, which attracted large audiences, had been closed off by the state of California, in the interests of decency. The village is a parody of the collection. In Mrs. Beauchamp's Parlour, which tries to imitate the decor of the most scandalous part of the collection, "young California girls wearing black lisle stockings and white cotton knickers with panels which opened to expose their behinds moved among the patrons, serving drinks and flaunting their breasts in provocative deshabille" (198). A menswear boutique is called Oscar Wilde Way Out, and the warehouse selling imitation Victorian knick-knacks is misleadingly named the Great Victorian Collection. The village is the "ultimate fake." However, the gullible public is eventually convinced that the warehouse is the Great Victorian Collection (198).

On a literal level, the novel's premise isn't as far-fetched as it appears to be. Take photocopying, for example. Technology has become so advanced that it can often be impossible to tell the difference between an original page of manuscript and a copy, unless we are informed by the author that one was printed from a disk and is the original, while the other is merely a copy. Of course, one might then inquire as to the status of that same page on a computer disk in relation to the document saved on the hard drive. Which is the original? In the future, it seems possible that copying and software will improve to the extent that it will be possible to re-create, for example, the Mona Lisa. This new work will not be a reproduction; it will be another "original." Of course, this will mean that there will be many "originals," that great works of art will be as common as televisions (one in every home), and that art will finally yield to democracy. On the flip side, the art market will collapse, great fortunes will be lost, nobody will be bothered going near art museums, and all of Sotheby's employees will be made redundant. Of course, such a scenario would never be allowed to unfold. Experts will make determinations and what is real will be separated from what is fake. Eco notes, in relation to books, that "the triumph of photocopying is creating a crisis in the publishing industry. Each of us if he can obtain, at less expense, a photocopy of a very expensive book avoids buying that book" (178).

With regard to postmodern fiction, Moore's removal of the Victoriana to a parking lot in California is similar to techniques used by both Cortazar and Nabokov in their fictions. Commenting on these writers, Brian McHale has noted:

> Similar effects are achieved by Julio Cortazar in his story "The Other Heaven" (from *All Fires the Fire and Other Stories*, 1966), where Buenos Aires of the 1940s is superimposed on Paris of the 1860s; and on a much larger scale in Nabokov's *Ada* (1970). The alternate world, or Antiterra,

of *Ada* has been constructed by superimposing Russia on the space occupied in our world by Canada and the United States, Britain on our France, Central Asia on European Russia, and so on. (47)

All three writers—Moore, Cortazar, and Nabokov—lived much of their lives outside their own countries. Imaginatively, they travel back and forth between where they were born and where they live until eventually locations travel too. Multiple locations are grafted together to make a single place which allows imaginative release, and which becomes a substitute homeland.

The issue of authenticity is a central concern in *The Great Victorian Collection* and the vehicle Moore uses to involve business, the mass media, and academe. A major contention is that the three are closely interdependent and self-serving. Business is represented by Management Incorporated, the creator of the Great Victorian Village. Management Incorporated, through its manipulation of the popular media, is remarkably successful in peddling its collection to the public. However, the more serious media, represented by the *New York Times,* and the nation's most incorruptible arbiters of veracity and taste, university experts, are not much concerned with unearthing the truth. The *New York Times* brings in H. F. Clews from Yale and Sir Alfred Mannings, the Director General of the British Imperial Collections, whose efforts cast doubt not only on the whole process of authenticating, but also on the presence of ethical standards, or the lack of such, in academe. This part of the novel is also extremely funny. Professor Clews is a man "with a port-wine nose" and believes that Maloney shouldn't be taken seriously as a scholar because his doctorate was received from a Canadian university and he is "insane" (53–54). Sir Alfred Mannings, a proud Briton with a low estimation of America, is horrified and "moved to indignation . . . to see these wonderful treasures laid out in flea-market fashion in an American car-park" (57). His reaction is comparable to that of Umberto Eco, who, when confronted by the objects present in the Hearst castle in San Simeon, notes that "what offends is the voracity of the selection, and what distresses is the fear of being caught up by this jungle of venerable beauties . . . redolent of contamination, blasphemy, [and] the Black Mass" (23). Mannings, although he is impressed by the collection, closes ranks with Clews and roundly condemns it as a fake to the *New York Times.*

To undo the damage done by the report in the *Times,* Management Incorporated brings in its own duo of experts:

There arrived that same afternoon Henry Prouse, Regius Professor of History at the University of Saskatchewan, and Charles Hendron, Keeper of the Dulwich Memorial Trust. Both were eminent Victorian scholars who had collaborated on a two volume work entitled *The Lodging Houses of Victorian London.* . . . Management Incorporated possessed an excellent research department. Some years before, *The Lodging Houses of Victorian London* had been reviewed unfavorably in the *Times Literary Supplement.* The unsigned review was written by Professor H. F. Clews of Yale. (86)

Naturally enough, given the animosity both scholars share for Clews, they are wild in their praise for the Carmel Collection. Hendron says that the "Carmel Collection is, without doubt, the greatest single collection of Victoriana to have been uncovered this century," while Prouse, in a flourish of hyperbole, proclaims that he has come into the presence of "perhaps the first wholly secular miracle in the history of mankind" (87). Neither duo of experts is much concerned with authenticity per se: The first is concerned with undermining Maloney, while the second seeks to settle an old score with the unfortunately named Clews. Of course, if one believes in the notion of universities as centers of disinterested learning where highly educated individuals seek the truth above all else, with little interest in money or fame, these passages of *The Great Victorian Collection* will be somewhat unnerving and lead one to grow as cynical about the motives of these people as about those of politicians.

Equally disturbing, but also delightfully funny, is how, by means of the introduction of a third expert, the evidence for authenticity is weighed. Lord Rennishawe is an eighty-one-year-old dwarf and the owner of Creechmore Castle in Wales who is able to verify the authenticity of many of the "lost" items (objects which once existed but were lost through time, fires, etc.). He tells a remarkable story of stumbling upon a room in an old summer house where his grandfather housed his sadistic equipment and paraphernalia. To this house, the grandfather lured young servant girls. Because of Rennishawe's titillating subject matter, he makes many appearances on television talk shows. Such appearances, and in view of both the media's power and America's love of aristocracy—Lord Rennishawe is, after all, the real thing—render the collection real in the eyes of the public. Until Rennishawe has made his round of the talk shows, Maloney's colleagues and superiors at McGill University are skeptical of his collection, are angered by his absence from work, and, in fact, remove him from his position; however, after Rennishawe has told his story, Maloney is reinstated.

Rennishawe's narrative is also remarkable for another reason. Not only is his story captivating, but it also is a good example of how well Moore uses the collection as material. Indeed it exists to indict experts, but it also takes on a life of its own. Each piece and part of the collection reflects some aspect of Victorian England and is fascinating in its own right.

Another process traced in the novel is how the creatorship and curatorship changes Maloney's life and eventually destroys him. In return for being granted the powers which enabled him to bring the collection into being, Maloney must forgo most of the elements which are part of a normal life—a job, a home, sexual relationships, the ability to enjoy food, and sleep. He must remain close to the collection, at the Sea Winds Motel. When he drives away from the collection with his secretary, Mary Ann McKelvey, to test whether items will be damaged by his absence, it rains, and damage is done. In another test, he tries to use his new powers to make the child's wooden fire engine move from the collection to his hotel bed. It does not move, but when he checks to see whether it is still in the collection, Maloney notices that it is no longer an original: It has become a cheap imitation bearing the inscription "Made in Japan."

> Then, and only then, Maloney realized the laws of this creation. Already the toy engine reproached him, a small cancerous blemish on the perfect bloom of the whole. It had been given to him to envisage the Collection here, in a parking lot in California. Any further attempts to remove these items to some other location would result, not in the greatest collection of Victoriana the world had ever seen, but in an astonishing conglomeration of Japanese fakes. (17)

Maloney is tied to Carmel by a Faustian pact. If he leaves, or tries to take the collection with him, it will become a greater fake than the Hearst Castle at San Simeon where at least some of the elements are real. Of course, Maloney travels to Los Angeles and Montreal because he wants to resist the vise of the powers which are imprisoning him, but is disconsolate on his return to discover the damage his absence has caused to the collection. He is torn between his desire to live a normal life, and his duty, as a scholar, to protect his collection. Does Moore suggest that the two are incompatible? In an effort to sleep without dreaming, because the collection also controls his dreams, Maloney takes to drinking hard and taking drugs in a vain attempt to induce forgetfulness and stupor. In addition, while in Montreal he cannot make satisfactory love to Mary Ann because he is not able to disassociate her from the collection, which is hundreds of miles away in Carmel.

One of the central themes explored by Moore throughout his career has been faith. In his world, it is difficult for the believer to have faith unless she or he is provided with some elements of the happy life. If none of these are provided, the individual will become unhappy and knotted with bitterness and rage. In *The Lonely Passion of Judith Hearne*, the main character calls on God in the tabernacle to reveal himself to her so she can confirm his presence, and her faith. She wants to be certain that there will be a bright future ahead for her when she leaves Belfast and this life, where she has been miserable. "'Show me a sign,'" she says (175). Even if the individual does not believe in a God or follow a religion, she or he is still possessed by a drive, which Jung refers to as "numinosum" in *Psychology and Religion,* that propels this person to find a substitute for a God, a person toward whom desire and the need for transcendence can be channeled (O'Donoghue, 154–55).

In *Cold Heaven* this process occurs in reverse: Marie Davenport is shown all the signs which are never revealed to Judith Hearne. Marie possesses beauty, wealth, and a husband—the elements of a happy life in Judith's view—but is unhappy and indifferent to the world and to religion. Yet an apparition of Our Lady appears to her near Carmel, where *The Great Victorian Collection* is set. Therefore, in two novels, two miracles take place within a few miles of each other, one secular, the other religious. Seamus Deane believes that in Moore's view "it is a radical dissatisfaction with the actual that leads in the end to either the acceptance of or the recognized possibility of a miracle" (*A Short History of Irish Literature,* 221).

Clearly, for Brian Moore, all modern America offers is shallowness, and it is the recognition of this by his protagonists which drives them to search for meaning, depth, and transcendence in either ultimate fakes, such as Disneyland and San Simeon, or in more traditional, but equally problematic, Catholic miracles. Also, both author and individual are forced by circumstances to consider the possibility that a God exists. Implicit in this turning toward the miraculous is the knowledge that attempts to find salvation through love affairs, marriages, and money have failed. In Moore's early Belfast novels, God and religion are oppressive, and both Judith Hearne and Diarmuid Devine (*The Feast of Lupercal*) seek liberation through the primal energies of this world—sex and love. In his American novels of the 1970s, Moore entertains the possibility that the opposite view is feasible: People are unable to make one another happy because, instead of cooperating, they compete against and exploit one another. Salvation, therefore, must come from outside, just as the preachers have been intoning for centuries. As a young man, Moore moved away from religious belief and embraced socialism because it appeared to lend itself to improving the lot of humankind, and it seemed more practical. However, as an older man, he is no longer able to accept that manipulation of the material world will lead to happiness, though he still does not seem to believe in a God or an afterlife.

As he grows older, Moore begins to distance himself from materialist philosophy and to move in the direction of the spiritual. As a writer, Moore is interested in exploring the gray areas which frequently define the lives of believers and unbelievers. The former are forced into crises when doubt undermines faith. For the latter, love of a man or woman is a substitute for love of God; when this love is undermined or broken, the individual is plunged into crisis. It is interesting to note that in *The Great Victorian Collection*, and other novels such as *I Am Mary Dunne*, *The Doctor's Wife*, *The Temptation of Eileen Hughes*, *Cold Heaven*, and *Lies of Silence*, it is the absence of satisfactory sexual relationships which leads to the collapse of marriages and relationships, even with God, such as what happens with Judith Hearne.

As was the case in *The Lonely Passion of Judith Hearne*, Moore's first novel, and in many that followed it, faith must be tested. In *The Great Victorian Collection*, this is achieved with great dexterity by Moore, again by bringing the collection into play.

The character Vaterman, like St. Thomas, does not quite believe in Maloney's abilities as a clairvoyant and seeks proof. One night, both he and Mary Ann hide in the collection and are discovered by Maloney, who "sensing that something was wrong," leaves his room and makes his way to a shed which contains the bedroom exhibit (89). Maloney is able to tell Vaterman exactly what items from the collection he has concealed in his pockets. Vaterman tells Maloney that he is a "genius," the modern equivalent of a God or saint.

Maloney's collapse is recorded by Dr. I. S. Spector of Vanderbilt University, who interviews him on a number of occasions and whose findings are published, after his death, in a long article in the *Journal of Parapsychology*. As Maloney disintegrates so does the collection, and in this respect Moore's novel begins to resemble Oscar Wilde's *The Picture of Dorian Gray*, and some techniques used by Alfred Hitchcock—for whom Brian Moore worked briefly—in his films and television dramas (Moore, interview by Eamonn Wall, 367–68). Eventually, Maloney's condition has deteriorated to such a degree that "the tour guides, if they saw him approach, would turn their groups into another aisle" (201). He tries to break an exhibit with a hammer; he attempts to set another on fire, and in the end kills himself.

What are we to make of all this? In her excellent book on Brian Moore, Jo O'Donoghue concludes that *The Great Victorian Collection* is a "fable that is never fully elucidated, an obscure parable about the nature of art and the possibility of miracles" (75). On one level, this is certainly true; however, it also misses the point because it tries to make of the novel what it is not. It is not fully elucidated because it is not fully a realist novel, but, rather, one written in the shadow of Borges, García Márquez, Barthelme, and Coover, and, as a consequence of the dominance of this mode of influence, must be obscure, and must be more concerned with its parts than with the whole. Such an approach seems ideal for a work whose subject is the fragmented and failed America which Moore finds outside his front door, as it were, in California—an America of fake objects and fake people bent on exploiting one another. Like Moore's other novels, it does not offer us much to take away with us in the form of conclusions, but rather a lot to ponder. Ultimately, I believe, *The Great Victorian Collection* is best read as a brilliantly constructed and ingeniously written book about the search for transcendence and faith in an America where both are on sale. To be sure, Moore is concerned with writers and their books and reviewers, but this is a secondary theme. Both Moore and Eco are writers who are simultaneously fascinated and repelled by America and whose visions are complex and confused, but irresistible.

In the first half of the twentieth century, Irish writers of fiction frequently spent much of their time outside Ireland, but wrote almost exclusively of Ireland. This is no longer the case, and no writer has blazed this trail more than Brian Moore. In this regard, and in many others as well, Moore has operated way ahead of his time and, despite his popularity and all the prizes and awards he has garnered for his fiction, has remained underestimated by critics. There are reasons for this. One is that he has written too many books, including some that are not good, and another is that his most popular and highly regarded novels are his most traditionally conceived, and these have not always appealed to high-brow arbiters of taste. His most innovative and daring novels, among which must be counted *The Great Victorian Collection* and *Cold Heaven,* are ground-breaking works in Irish writing, but not, as yet, accepted as such. Perhaps Moore's multiple identities—Irish-born and raised, Canadian passport-holder, and California resident—have hindered his ability to be tidily packaged for consumers. Ironically, these same multiple identities are central to Moore's artistic consciousness and a consistent source of strength. In recent years, many Irish novelists have followed Moore's example and written about America—Sebastian Barry in *The Engine of Owl-Light* and Colum McCann in *Songdogs,* to name but two excellent examples. It is certain that the trend will continue, for Irish writers will always be drawn toward America, because America is an extension of Ireland, and will follow Brian Moore by writing about it. But, even though they will continue to find America strange, they will find it a great challenge to describe it as well as Brian Moore does in *The Great Victorian Collection.*

Eleven

How Decent People Live
Thomas McGonigle's *Going to Patchogue*

In *Going to Patchogue,* his second novel, Thomas McGonigle traces the return of a man nearing forty (also called Thomas McGonigle) to his hometown, Patchogue, Long Island, in a futile attempt at self-discovery. He hopes not only to reconstruct, by means of personal, political, and social history, a town and its people, but also to resolve a number of conflicts within himself. He wants to discover the extent to which his early life in Patchogue has contributed to the person he is now, and to see to what degree the Patchogue he recalls corresponds to the present one.

The visit yields no answers. At its end (when the traveler has returned to his home in New York City), he admits: "Myself has come back. I am in the City. I have gone to Patchogue. I have been in Patchogue. I have come back from Patchogue" (212). He feels as Joyce did after his final visit home to Dublin:

> "I find it difficult to come to any other conclusion but this—that the intention was to weary me out and if possible strangle me once and for all. But in this they did not succeed." (quoted in Ellmann, 337)

On the novel's final page is a photograph taken in the Patchogue train station. In the center of it is a sign telling the commuter/traveler that he or she is in Patchogue. Underneath the town's name are two arrows—one pointing to New York, the other to "Points East." The town is simultaneously an entity in itself, but also a place from which one leaves for other places. Each morning the residents of the town board the Long Island Railroad for jobs in the city and in the evening they return home. The town boasts of having the largest railroad parking lot on Long Island, which strengthens the notion that the town has no self-sustaining soul of its own, since its parking lot is its most famous landmark.

The narrator of this novel has also followed the arrows in the train station: In addition to his westward journey to New York City, he has traveled eastward to Ireland, Bulgaria, and Turkey. On his return, he real-izes that he cannot view Patchogue independently, but is forced to see it as part of the wider experiences he has garnered in other places. Although he is still obsessed by painful memories of unrequited love for Melinda, his high school sweetheart, he finds that when he tries to recall her she becomes blended with other blonde women he has encountered in other places. Because he can gather no clear view of the Patchogue he knew as a child and because the experiences he has had in places beyond it have not been satisfactory, he returns to the city full of despair and gloom.

Like his earlier novel *The Corpse Dream of N. Petkov* (1987), *Going to Patchogue* is concentrated and complex. In *Petkov*, McGonigle fo-cused on the final minutes of the Bulgarian patriot's life and wove from that short period of time, by examining past and present, a dense personal and historical fabric. In *Going to Patchogue*, the author uses a similar construction, though here, because a day rather than a few minutes is allotted to the work, the novel is twice as long. Nevertheless, despite the greater length, *Going to Patchogue* is also a concentrated work. Instead of producing a monumentally long novel like *Ulysses*, McGonigle has in-stead produced a marvelously resonant shorter work, one which operates on the principal of leaving out rather than putting in. However, the con-sistently high quality of the prose and McGonigle's ability to select the most telling details from his knowledge of Patchogue contributes to the novel's effect. Of course, McGonigle is also the author of the splendid but unpublished "St. Patrick's Day 1974," a monumental one-day-in-Dublin novel, chapters of which have appeared in journals such as the *Review of Contemporary Fiction*.

Michael Stephens's *Season at Coole* is a starting point for Thomas McGonigle, the novel which prodded him to write *Going to Patchogue*. In his afterword to the reissued version of Stephens's novel, McGonigle notes:

> I read *Season at Coole* as a confirmation of my own experience, of the worth of my own experience. Because of the clarity of Stephens's vision I was able to see my own experience more fully, to see the similarities, to see the differences, possibly because truth resides in the rescued de-tails. . . . With Stephens I am taken right into the centrality of my nervous system and am allowed again to feel, to know, the taste of sour ash. (174)

Although *Season at Coole* has much to recommend it, it is hardly the ambitious and complex novel (thematically, formally, and intellectually) that *Going to Patchogue* is. The mature Michael Stephens emerges in two magnificent works published in 1994: the novel *The Brooklyn Book of the Dead*, which is a sequel to *Season at Coole*, and the collection of

essays *Green Dreams: Essays Under the Influence of the Irish.* Where
Stephens focuses on a single family as representative of the role and faith
of Irish America in suburbia, McGonigle seeks to describe suburbia itself,
and to examine it in relation to contemporary America as a whole.
McGonigle, as James McCourt has pointed out, employs the "laborious
methods of archeology—teaspoons and sifters—to lay truth bare."

Patchogue's natives are not always enlightened or likable. For the most
part, they are lower-middle-class Irish Americans who have "escaped"
from New York City and settled in Patchogue in an attempt to find some
form of suburban paradise. Most of them are convinced that Patchogue
is superior to New York City, and one man berates McGonigle for leaving
Patchogue, spending so much time outside of the United States, and settling down in the City on his return:

> I stayed here and you left. You don't know how decent people behave,
> living all those years away from this country and then living in the City.
> How do you expect to know how decent people live if all you do is associ-
> ate with foreigners and City People?
>
> Your father was a City Person, I said.
>
> And so was yours . . . but they got themselves out of the City. What
> can you find in the City . . . just disease, I'll tell you, disease and prepara-
> tion for disease. (99)

They are unnerved by the knowledge that the city is spreading out and
encroaching on their paradise, that the people they have fled have suddenly and nightmarishly reappeared on their doorsteps. Such comments
are typical of what is heard in Patchogue, where narrow-mindedness, usually manifested in racist and xenophobic statements, is widespread. From
the smaller canvas of *Season at Coole,* one might assume that hatred of
nonwhites and non-Christians was an Irish American preserve; however,
after reading *Going to Patchogue* one suspects that these attitudes are
widespread in all suburban communities on Long Island. By so indicating, McGonigle certainly adds fuel to the fire of bad publicity Long Island
has received in recent times. But what is also clear from McGonigle's portrait is that the suburbs are more an extension of the city than separate
entities in themselves, and that the city has encroached on Patchogue with
the result that both share similar problems. It is unnecessary for the residents of McGonigle's Patchogue to re-create the city in their own domains, as the Cooles do: If it can't be found on their own blocks, it will
be found down the street and around the corner. McGonigle, in his treat-
ment of these people, emerges as one of the few white writers with the
courage to portray white racists as they are. Many white intellectuals
when they consider such tragic events as the Howard Beach affair and the

murder of Yousef Hawkins will argue that these crimes were aberrations which in no way reflected the views of the majority of whites. But McGonigle, on the other hand—and I am inclined to agree with him— suggests that racism is part of the psychological make-up of all white people. In this instance, and in many others in the novel, McGonigle is honest and brave.

Going to Patchogue is a collage. It is part travelogue and part meditation on traveling home, and on travel in general; it is part personal history and part the history of Patchogue from its founding to the present. It is a deeply personal and painful work, but also one which will appeal to all Americans who have moved away from their roots (most of the nation, I suspect), but who have at one time or another returned there in the hope of resurrecting some part of the lost essences of place and self. Both the traveler's despair and the town are brought convincingly to life.

The novel has three parts. In the first, the narrator is in his Greenwich Village apartment contemplating the journey he is about to make. In the second, he is in Patchogue. In the third, he is on a Long Island Railroad car returning to the city from the island. What one is presented with is a many-layered portrait whose layers accumulate as one progresses through the work. In this way the narrator's teenage infatuation for Melinda is described, as are events remembered from childhood—concerning himself, his parents, and many unsavory, and some comic, episodes from village life. It is Melinda, however, who is the source of the deepest resonances:

> I am not going to tramp down to the Shorefront Park and stand in the outfield waiting for the fly ball that will never be hit my way, because they know, just stand there out in right field underneath the tall night lightpole and wait, wait, wait, and just over there in the front of ceremonial boulder I took Melinda's photograph and that photograph is wrapped in some sort of plastic covering. I watch it yellow and orange to disappear, destroying the image, eating it up as if it were in a burst of orange and yellow, a mockery of my heart's ache which now must travel to new places and never, never will it beat faster, never will it leap to the idea of possibility. (95)

Before leaving New York City, the narrator provides us with some facts about Patchogue (this calls to mind the opening of *Moby Dick*): that it has been visited at various times by such luminaries as George Washington, Thoreau, Irving Berlin, P. G. Wodehouse; is fifty-eight miles from New York City and sixty-nine from Montauk; that "Patchogue is first in Suffolk County in the number of parking spaces in the downtown area"; and so on (7). Information is culled from a variety of sources—newspa-

pers, history books, and encyclopedias. In a humorous vein, the village
clerk is quoted:

> Patchogue sordid? "Oh, not at all," said Village Clerk Rose Marie Ber-
> ger. "I think of Patchogue as one of the most progressive villages on the
> South Shore of Long Island. We have a great water front with recreational
> facilities. We have a dynamic business district. We have a terrific sewer sys-
> tem. In snowstorms, our streets are cleared. We have back door sanitation
> pickup so you don't have to put your garbage pails in front of the house.
> We were one of the first villages with a recycling program. Now that re-
> cycling is mandatory, everyone is jumping in." (15)

McGonigle, in an attempt to understand who he is on the day he journeys to Patchogue, wrestles with his multiple identities: literate city-
dweller, child of suburbia, American, Irish American, and so on. He sets
out for Patchogue as a stranger and returns none the wiser, though he
realizes that "he [doesn't] have to travel to Patchogue to be there. He is
always in Patchogue," and declares that he will not return again (42).
While on this brief trip, he recalls extended periods of time spent in Istan-
bul, Sofia, and Dublin, and begins to understand that these intervals
could possibly be more significant than his childhood in Patchogue. Certainly, these foreign cities are presented as being more attractive, and free
of the intellectual poverty he notices in his home village on Long Island.

As an author, McGonigle could perhaps claim to be a Bulgarian American writer, having lived there for a few years and having published *The
Corpse Dream of N. Petkov*, which deals with political events which occurred after World War II. What McGonigle suggests, I believe, is that it
is possible (as a result of travel) for the writer to migrate from one background to another and develop a hybrid imagination:

> How did we end up in this place? Bulgaria. How did I end up in this
> place? Probably in vain, asking this question as once on Mount Desert Is-
> land, looking down into the harbor, seeing the yachts and complaining
> about being born in Brooklyn . . . but at least you are alive, Mom replies,
> unlike your brother who only saw one day of life. (170)

Life, therefore, instead of being rooted in the idea of home, becomes a
complex series of negotiations between different pasts and selves. The
only aspect of life to be mourned is the very early years in Brooklyn: Because these cannot be remembered, they are lost.

However, from his work as the founder and editor of the Irish and Irish
American journal *Adrift*, it is clear that Irish and European writing have
influenced McGonigle greatly. In particular, the voices of outsiders such
as Francis Stuart and Celine register sharply in *Going to Patchogue*. Also

influential is the Irish novelist Aidan Higgins, on whose work McGonigle has published a long essay. Higgins, too, has traveled widely and returned to Ireland to find it "extraordinarily empty" (*Balcony of Europe*, 457).

When one meets the unpleasant characters in the Oasis Bar and elsewhere in Patchogue, one is reminded of similar situations and individuals in Higgins's work: of the vulgar men whose conversations Helen Langrishe overhears on the bus from Dublin to County Kildare in *Langrishe, Go Down,* and of the many men and women (locals and foreigners) who appear in the Spanish section of *Balcony of Europe,* particularly the Baron from Balticum, whose hatred of Jews echoes the hatred of African Americans which is dramatized in Patchogue's Oasis Bar.

When we think of emigration, immigration, and migration, we enter a complex field which encompasses, to cite a few examples, not only the diasporas from Ireland and mainland Europe, but also the movement of people from the Eastern United States across the country to the West, and the more recent migrations from the cities to the suburbs, about which McGonigle and Michael Stephens are concerned. It is certainly interesting to note that McGonigle has returned to Ireland to unearth singular elements of style which he has grafted to his distinctive voice and vision. *Going to Patchogue* is an original, disturbing, and beautifully written novel by an emerging master of the form.

Twelve

The Black Hills, the Gorey Road, and Object Lessons

We did not ask you white men to come here. The Great Spirit gave us this country as a home. You had yours. We did not interfere with you.
—Crazy Horse (Lakota)

Going back is a lesson in proportion, an exercise in give-and-take, more revelation than deja vu.
—William Trevor (Irish)

My children were asleep and my wife was inside reading on a bed, while I was sitting outside of our rental cabin in a campground a few miles outside Custer, South Dakota. It was the longest day of the year and the evening was cloudless and cool, the sky enormous in one direction and blocked by pine trees on another. I was a long way from home, aware all day as I drove westward of the widening gap between where I was now and where I had left on my American journey, begun twelve years before when I had loaded suitcases into a car and headed for Dublin airport.

But I was so happy: Since childhood I had dreamed of driving across America but doubted if I'd ever get the opportunity to accomplish it. As kids, we referred to General Custer as General "Custard," which made him familiar to us, and this was one silly thing which occurred to me this afternoon when we rolled into Custer, the town.

We had driven here from Omaha, where we live now, so we had not come far; however, each of us, in our own way, as the radio served a steady diet of Patsy Cline and Hank Williams, felt the impact of the miles, markers, and the steady rising movement toward the hills. The West had begun to become a presence we could feel. Somewhere west of Valentine we had crossed into a new and sacred territory. To a degree, I'd been prepared for this: two sentences from Kathleen Norris's *Dakota: A Spiritual Geography* had been running round and round in my head for a couple of weeks. The first went like this: "Nature, in Dakota, can indeed be an experience of the holy" (1). The second followed thus: "The sense of place is un-

109

avoidable in western Dakota, and maybe that's our gift to the world" (169). I suppose it was this book more than anything else which inspired my visit. I wished to view for myself this "holy" landscape, experience this "holiness" first-hand, and measure it against "the holy ground" of Ireland which I knew so well. Also, I wanted to drive to Dakota and witness "sense of place" in a topography I felt strangly drawn to, but for which I felt singularly unprepared. In Ireland, place, personality, and identity are inseparable; however, I doubted whether the Irish emotional lens through which I observed the world—the narrow street, the small field, the wet grass—could accommodate these huge, dry vistas located in the center of the continent.

In this frame of mind, I arrived. A few hours earlier, we had been delayed because the main road was blocked by construction. We took a secondary route and got blocked there too. A Native American woman directing traffic with a stop/go sign told me to drive back a few miles and turn onto a dirt road which would connect with the main road beyond where the other crew was working, so I followed her directions—I went back, and turned left, and proceeded slowly up the winding dirt road, over the red earth of the Black Hills. It was an extraordinary, and quite accidental, experience—to be in the dark center of a forest in the middle of a continent, in a white station wagon with my wife and children. When we stopped the car, which we did frequently, I listened to the sound of the breeze blowing the low-lying branches of the evergreens and felt the cool air coming from the forest into the car and touching our mesmerized faces. Above the road was the brightness of a sky without clouds, and to each side the great darkness and mystery of the forest.

I remained quiet. I listened to the excited voices of my wife and children, who were in awe of this opportunity to be in this place, which chance had presented. I knew, too, because similar events in my own childhood had transfixed me, that my children were learning the language of the landscape of their country. My wife, as she watched and spoke, understood that she had come home to her people and her own childhood; it was the trees which told her this. I felt the mystery, power, and gravitational pull of sacred ground. What seemed so important to me was the knowledge that my children were finding their places in their own landscape, as I had found mine in the County Wexford of my childhood.

Two years before, I had brought them out of New York City and placed them on the American prairie; it concerned me that I had stolen their sense of belonging to a place. I felt I had. But this morning I understood I'd delivered them to another. Instead of belonging to just one place—something which strongly afflicts me—they had now inherited a sense of belonging to multiple places and a healthy attitude toward the world. I had brought them away from the superficial, in a sense, toward the center of place. Thomas Merton has described life as an inward journey; I understood that we had arrived at this inward place where, perhaps, we are meant to bury that oar. Here was a day, here were the parts of a day, so important and unforgettable. For once, because parenthood allowed me to be both observer and participant, I was able to know history as it happened and not just as memory. As a father, I have been taught by nature that my own desires—my life, in fact—is secondary to my children's; therefore, I have been freed from self to become facilitator and observer.

But it was also possible, perhaps even likely, that the intensity experienced on that longest day in the Black Hills represented a certain apex in my life as husband and parent.

The feeling was one which mixed joy and sorrow: We had reached a fork in the road at which we separated—three going in one direction, myself in another, and it seemed to me that I was about to begin the immigrant experience all over again. By bringing them to the center of their landscape, I was reminded of the distance separating me from my own. At the same time, I had given a wife, a son, and a daughter the gift of the country they had been born to. Were all of these—love, marriage, fatherhood—mere coincidences or connected to fate? It seemed quite wonderful to me that I, a stranger and an immigrant, was the one who had guided my wife and children to the center of *their* native land. To be happy in the world you must feel that you have ventured out from some place called home which has filled you with what we call sense of place and which has given you the confidence to continue with your travels. For them, the Black Hills was one such starting point.

Suddenly, after rounding a corner, we found our way blocked by a buffalo. My son told me that they are called bison, that buffalo is incorrect. I couldn't believe how big it was, how slowly it walked. I had been trained as a driver in rural Ireland, so was used to sharing the road with animals. Still, this was a new experience and I wasn't sure how to react. If I drove up close behind the animal and honked the horn, would he run off into the forest, or would he rear up in anger and damage the car? In the Irish scenario, there would have been many animals—sheep or cattle—but also a farmer and his dog. In the end, we turned the car around to find the point where we had left the blacktop and joined the dirt road. We turned back because of what my fellow travelers agreed on: The buffalo owned the forest and the dirt road, so it was for us to yield, not him. A short while later, we passed the point where the woman had stood directing traffic and where the men had been working on the road. Not only had the crew departed, but there was no sign at all of the road even having

been opened and new tarmac laid. It was as if this crew had been spirits
sent to direct us to the dirt road, the forest, and the buffalo.

America is a huge and complex country. As a child growing up in Ireland,
I understood it to be simpler than Ireland. Now I know it would take
many lifetimes to uncover its mysteries, beauties, and divisions. But on
that evening in the campground outside Custer, I wasn't interested in
working hard on those difficult issues. Instead, I sat in the pure peace-
fulness of evening full of the whooping joy of arrival—watching, breathing, opening up like a flower. On the road that morning, somewhere between Valentine and Chadron in the Nebraska Sandhills, I was reminded
of another road—the one which connects my hometown of Enniscorthy,
County Wexford, with the small seaside village of Courtown. My father
is at the wheel of a Ford Cortina, which is full of children. This road and
these names are a mantra for me framing my childhood. As I have driven
other roads in cars or buses, or looked out the windows of trains, or sat
alone in airports waiting to board a plane, I have often been reminded of
the feelings of exultation sparked by the pulling away of the family car
from the curb in Enniscorthy and the beginning of the brief, yet enormous
and mythical trip from town to seaside.

Each road I travel repeats, recalls, defines, refines, and returns me to
that one road and that singular world of childhood. My mind wanders
backward: I note the garages which frame one side of the Island Road,
then St. Mary's Graveyard where my grandparents are buried, then the
ditches alive with daisies, primroses, and wild fuschia fighting for light
through the briars, and the barley-rich fields of the Model County. On
pasture land, cows graze quietly or loll in the summer sun. I remember,
on the old road through Blackstoops, the exact point where a table was
set on which were placed strawberries and honeycombs for sale, and I
remember once, in the back of the car, tearing into a comb with my fingers and teeth (like a bear in a cartoon) before passing it on to my brother
for his turn. At Scarawalsh, the road divides: one way, the sea; the other,
Bunclody and the mountains. Then Ferns, the ancient capital of Leinster
and the seat of Diarmuid MacMurrough, who brought the Normans to
Ireland. Along the wide stretch of road outside Ferns, near the Halal meat
plant, are large banked fields full of sheep, and to the east, the railway
line. Then Camolin, then the shopfronts of Gorey—McCormack's, the
64, French's, O'Connor's, Hurney's, Cooke's, and Webb's—and the town
full of Saturday shoppers. As we enter Courtown, we see, to our right,
the ballroom and, above us, the sea. We turn right and, when the car
stops, jump out and abandon our father to the bags and boxes.

For travel and me, there's always existed the instantly recognizable moment of arrival. As a child on my way to the seaside, this might occur outside Camolin, after we had turned to the right off the main road and begun to make our way toward the sea by the back road under old trees which stretched across the road forming shadows and tunnels. Here was a narrow, magical way of light and shade, houses and fields, cars and pheasants. Other times, the moment was revealed as I sat in the parked car before leaving town. Perhaps, as Baudelaire reminds us, it is the act of traveling which counts and not the destination:

> But the true voyagers are those who leave
> Only to be going; hearts nimble as balloons,
> They never diverge from luck's black sun,
> And with or without reason, cry, Let's be gone!
> "The Voyage," 1367

On that evening in South Dakota, my heart had slowed and my will retreated. I had arrived. On another continent, I had re-created a journey made in childhood. I looked across at the trees and tried to imagine what journeys my chidren would make when they were grown and wondered what they might remember of our coming to the Black Hills. What I lacked that night was a sense of history. As a child driving from Enniscorthy to Courtown, I was crossing a landscape and a history which I felt I understood, if I didn't quite. Of the Black Hills I knew little. Visually, all previous experiences had left me unprepared for them. Of my knowledge of its history, I knew this: If I examined it, I would be shown that almost everything I had picked up previously was wrong.

Many afternoons as children during the Christmas holidays, my friends and I showed up for the afternoon matinee at the Astor Cinema in Enniscorthy. We were between the ages of seven and ten, so it must have spanned the years from 1962 to 1966. Most of us had no televisions at home during that period; therefore, the cinema represented a vital outlet, was an important contact with the outside world, and was excitement personified. Two movies were shown each afternoon; we went on days old westerns were shown. The slick new releases, in which John Wayne appeared in color, were shown at night and were more expensive. These movies represented my first visual contact with America; whatever familiarity I developed with America was gleaned from such movies, or pictures, as we used to call them. I don't recall reading any books about America during childhood; instead, I read about British war heroes since these books were readily available and fairly inexpensive. I'm sure that the county library had plenty of books about America; however, I was unable to enter it since I had failed to return a previously borrowed book and feared the wrath of the librarian. At that time, one didn't read Irish children's books, except in school, since none were available, at least not in the country. Until the middle of the 1970s, when news agents expanded their stocks, it was difficult to buy books in rural Irish towns. As a result, despite the election, the Irish visit, and the assassination of President Kennedy, America was remote from me. I was the product of an Ireland that was rich, intense, and quite wonderful—except for primary school—but which was isolated. With the benefit of improved communication and Ireland's place in the international economic community, the generations who grew up in the 1970s and 1980s have a much greater sense of what is happening in America. They know America, or feel they do, whereas we hadn't a clue beyond what appeared on the movie screen. I can't recall ever meeting an American as a child, and I stayed away from television, which was dominated by American programs, since the medium didn't appeal to me.

We brought our cap guns and cowboy paraphrenalia with us to the Astor Cinema. Quickly, we identified who the enemy was in the movie and started blasting away. The cachophony in the cinema was beyond belief: a couple of hundred guns blasting and plenty of shouting and stomping of feet. This was an innocent time in Ireland—before the "troubles" resumed in the North. But I remember growing out of this sort of entertainment—at the age of ten or so—when someone got the board game Risk for Christmas and when our gang learned how to play Bridge. But it remained true and unaltered that the first visual sight of America to fill my imagination was provided by Hollywood. At times, in high excitement, the Slaney became the Rio Grande and the Bare Meadows the desert. The cowboys and Indians were cartoon characters with the former generally the good guys—they looked like us and were Christians—and the latter the bad—they looked and acted like heathens. Clearly, these movies were underlined by a not-too-subtle racism which I didn't notice at the time since I was too young, or naive, or both.

The Black Hills were formed "in the Pleistocene upheaval that brought forth the Rockies . . . and [form] a remote ridge of granite and limestone—one hundred miles by forty—soaring over the surrounding landscape, basking in their peculiar isolation, and commanding a vast arc of the plain below" (Lazarus, 3). For centuries, these mountains and surrounding lands had been the home to the Kiowa, Hidatsa, and the Mandan; however, these were supplanted by the Sioux, who had crossed the Missouri River in search of a new homeland after being hounded out of their own lands by the Chippewa, their ancient enemy, in what was later to become Minnesota. The Chippewa, who lived to the east of the Sioux, and closer to areas the white men inhabited, acquired guns from the Europeans, which resulted in their supremacy over the Sioux. Eventually, the Sioux too were armed with guns, and this, in tandem with their adept use of horses, made them the dominant power in their new homeland, which includes much of modern-day North Dakota, South Dakota, Iowa, and Nebraska. While in Minnesota, the Sioux were settled but, with the move westward, they followed the buffalo in spring and summer and camped during the late fall and winter months. The Sioux who inhabited the Black Hills were the Tetons, comprising the Oglala, Brule, Hunkpapa, Miniconjous, Sans Arc, Two Kettle, and Blackfeet (Lazarus, 4). But we must be careful with these names: Clearly, many of them are French and it would be more proper, for example, to use *Sicangu* instead of Brule. In his book *In the Spirit of Crazy Horse*, Peter Matthiessen quotes John Fire Lame Deer:

> "Our people don't call themselves Sioux or Dakota. That's white man talk. We call ourselves *Ikce Wicasa*—the natural humans, the free, wild, common people. I am pleased to be called that." (xxv)

One cannot overestimate the importance of the Black Hills to the Sioux. Although they have inhabited them for a comparatively short period of time, nevertheless the hills have become the physical and spiritual promised land to which the Sioux have been delivered. At the top of a flyer, which I found on the Internet, for Mel Lawrence's film *Paha Sapa* (meaning "Black Hills" in Lakota), the following statement appears:

> The Black Hills of South Dakota are to the Lakota Sioux and Cheyenne Indians what Mount Sinai is to the Jews, the Vatican is to the Roman Catholics, and Mecca is to the Muslims. Sacred to the Indian—but not to the white man—the Black Hills have come to symbolize the misappropriation of Indian lands by the U.S. government. ("Native Peoples," website)

The great Hunkpapa Sioux chieftain Sitting Bull declared that "God made me an Indian and put me here, *in this place*" (Cook-Lynn, 88). The hills are the home to *Wakan Tanka*, the Great Spirit, and "as an old Teton chief remembered: 'according to a tribal legend these hills were a reclining female figure from whose breasts flowed life-giving forces and to them the [Teton] went as a child to its mother's arms'" (Lazarus, 8).

When I read the history books and learned of the level of the injustice inflicted on the native people (then and now) by the United States, I forgot, for a while, all about the spiritual power of the Black Hills. I read that the great leaders Crazy Horse and Sitting Bull, who had defeated

Custer at the Battle of Little Big Horn on June 25, 1876, were both murdered, years later, after surrendering to the United States; that Big Foot and his followers were massacred at Wounded Knee by U.S. forces, after they had handed over their weapons, on December 29, 1890; that Indian children were forcibly educated in U.S. schools to ensure that they would lose their own language and culture; that religious rites, such as the Ghost Dance, were proscribed; and that lands were taken away "in exchange" for reservations. I read of dire poverty, lack of adequate health care, and of the general air of hopelessness which pervades Pine Ridge Reservation, where Wounded Knee is located, in South Dakota. I read the accounts of the occupation of Wounded Knee by the American Indian Movement in 1973, which pitted a small armed group of Indian activists, led by Russell Means and Dennis Banks, against the firepower and resources of the United States, the greatest military and ecomomic power the world has ever known; and the arrest, trial, and incarceration of Leonard Peltier for a crime that remains unproven.

Why do I find these accounts so shocking and disturbing? Certainly they undermine the view of America presented by the movies I saw in the Astor Cinema in Enniscorthy as a child, but a long time ago I had learned that that vision was false, that Hollywood presented the West as a cartoon with "real people." No, it's more than this. As an adult, I had built up an idea of the romance of America—generated by books, music, and the imagination—which was generally positive. In itself, within its own borders, the United States represented an idea and a movement toward a benign resolution of its difficulties; there was a feeling that things would be worked out. My visit to the Black Hills has not only forced me to examine the concerted attempts by the United States to exterminate the Indians, but it has also made me think again of slavery; of the Civil Rights Movement; of the assassinations of Dr. King, the Kennedys, Lincoln, John Lennon; of the Vietnam War; of the Rodney King trial; and to question my earlier assumptions. I am reminded of the limitations of my own reading and experience, and of how important it is to leave the library or office, venture out into the country or onto the streets, and ask such hard questions as: What are the impulses which have made America what it is—the common good, racism, or what?

But America, you know, is so seductive. The other evening, I sat outside on the steps for an hour or so watching a few kids ride their bikes up and down our street. I heard their joyful cries and their screeching brakes. Earlier in the day, it had rained so heavily and powerfully—with thunder, lightning, and tornado warnings to the north—that now both the peace and the peculiar late orange light were overwhelming. I looked at the high silver maples, the well-kept lawns, and the long, straight, endless American footpaths I have come to like so much, and wanted to be frozen in this spot forever. It's easy to separate the personal from the political and the historical. In this instance, one of the children is mine; he has just learned how to ride a bike. Yet my Irish childhood confirmed that for us—Irish people—such separations are impossible. In America, on the other hand, where progress and reinvention are pursued with such vigor, history is effectively filed and shelved like the old checks returned by the bank.

At the root of much of the trouble in the Black Hills is the second Fort Laramie Treaty of 1868, signed between the Lakota nation and the United States, "which recognized Lakota sovereignty in their Dakota-Wyoming homelands and hunting grounds, including the sacred Paha Sapa, the Black Hills" (Matthiessen, xx). In 1873, after gold was discovered in the Black Hills, the United States broke the treaty by illegally annexing much of the lands which fell under the aegis of the Fort Laramie Treaty and began the process of confining the Lakota to shrinking reservations on the poorest land. After a battery of legal challenges, the United States Supreme Court, in a landmark judgment, ruled in favor of the Lakota. The Lakota, at the conclusion of the longest running claim in American legal history, were awarded more than $106 million in compensation and interest for the loss of the Black Hills. The court announced its decision on June 30, 1980, fifty-seven years after Ralph Case filed the Black Hills claim (Lazarus, 401). In the end, after much debate, the Lakota rejected the settlement. As Edward Lazarus points out, the monetary award was not as large as it appeared: If it were distributed on a per capita basis, each claiment would receive only $1500. Nevertheless, it surprised many that the inhabitants of some of the poorest areas in the United States were willing to reject such a large sum of money. However, the settlement was rejected for reasons which had nothing to do with money: "I cannot accept money for the Black Hills," Severt Young Bear, an activist, explained,

> "because land is sacred to me. . . . [The whites] are trying to change our value system. To be a traditional person is to believe in your own culture, is to believe in yourself as a Lakota person; then you cannot sell the land."
> (Lazarus, 405)

Over time, some Lakota have felt that the settlement should have been accepted and the money invested in worthwhile enterprises. Maria Cudmore, the Cheyenne River Treasurer, believed that "with the world situation being what it is today, it would be futile to think we would ever get the Black Hills back" (Lazarus, 405). To this day, the settlement monies are lodged in a bank and continue to earn interest, while the U.S. Supreme

Court has refused to hear motions which call for the return of the Black Hills to the Lakota with compensation for resources such as gold and uranium that have been extracted from the land.

One factor that excited me the most about leaving Ireland for America was that my new home offered the possibility of escape from history. Certainly, to have grown up in the midst of ruins and old battlefields was exciting and a spur to the imagination. I grew up with the sense that my home area was important in both Irish and European history. As a child when I read history or listened to a teacher recite it like a poem in school, I listened carefully. Eventually, despite going on to study it in college, I grew disillusioned with it. History, I had begun to think, cluttered the landscape and cast a smokescreen over Irish life which hid other important and less "heroic" aspects of Ireland. What was the point of history, I wondered, if all it did was, as a result of sectarian violence, induce hatred and leave children of the North without fathers or mothers? In America, I thought, I would be outside history and without a care. America, from my vantage point in Ireland, was new and unburdened by a lot of monuments to battle sites, monastic ruins, and the like. Also, I would have the opportunity to live in a country as an outsider, to not belong if I chose. I didn't feel I had to care. I had no voting rights. But what landscapes and the humans and animals that populate them do is draw you into history; that hill over there, after all, has a name and a story to be told. Wherever I go, I am drawn toward the human voice. I am a good listener. When I traveled to the Black Hills, I was drawn into history. There was nothing I could do about it, and I felt the landscape invite me: first to listen, then to read, and, finally, to speak.

It is not easy to speak, however, because, inevitably, I will be tempted to explore the common ground between the experience of the Irish and the Lakota. It is easy to be drawn into fallacy, to feel, as it were, that because one has lived one life, one understands another. Yet certain issues—of land, language, identity, religion, culture—make our histories comparable. Also, such terms as genocide and colonization can be used in discussions of both. What makes me reluctant to draw conclusions are the writings of two Native American poets, Elizabeth Cook-Lynn and Wendy Rose, and scenes from *Rattle and Hum,* the documentary movie of a U2 tour.

After watching the band perform "I Still Haven't Found What I'm Looking For" with a Harlem choir, I was angry: I felt U2 was using the singers and the neighborhood to make the song seem more authentic, to suggest that the experiences of rich Irish rock stars and the people of Harlem were the same. What right had U2 to make such assumptions? None, in my book. But they had the money, and plenty of it I'm sure, to pay the singers, to buy authenticity. A result of this, of course, was that the movie was so widely disseminated that many viewers left the cinema thinking that they had encountered *truth*. However, on another level, I understood that U2 was traveling to the source of music to pay homage to its roots, to show, in their duet with B.B. King, and in their performance of Bob Dylan's "All Along the Watchtower," how deeply Irish lives had been molded by these profound voices. Bridges between Ireland and America, they are reminding us, allow for traffic to move in both directions; however, we must tread modestly and carefully.

Wendy Rose finds that white American artists, in the general sense, have used and abused Native American art in similar ways. She quotes the Lakota scholar Vine Deloria, Jr., who wrote that "the realities of Indian belief and existence have become so misunderstood and distorted at this point that when a real Indian stands up and speaks the truth at any given moment, he or she is not only unlikely to be believed, but will probably be contradicted and 'corrected' by the citation of some non-Indian and totally inaccurate 'expert'" (quoted in Rose, 404). Sometimes, when underprepared yet well-intentioned American "experts" discuss Ireland, I am struck by the fact that these speakers do not believe Ireland to be a culturally separate entity but rather see it as an extension of the United States. These experts, who give Irish Studies a bad name, have learned in seminar rooms the rudiments of Jungian theory, colonialism, postcolonialism, and so on, and feel equipped to understand every other place because, in their view, one place is pretty much the same as the next: Pine Ridge, the Bogside, Soweto, and Kinshasa are interchangeable. At such times, I have felt that my experience of growing up in Ireland, of feeling so bound to its soil that I could taste it in my mouth, is a thing without currency or value. Keeping these things in mind, I asked myself: Why should I raise my voice on the subject of the Black Hills? It's certainly not needed. Too many whites have misunderstood Native American culture; why should I add my name to the list?

As do Wendy Rose and the other Native American writers I have read subsequent to my visit to the Black Hills, Elizabeth Cook-Lynn writes a straightforward and angry narrative. Her stridency reinforces in my mind the weakness of literary theory and the distance which separates the seminar room from the field. For Cook-Lynn, as a member of the Crow Creek Sioux tribe, a poet, and an activist, it is neither desirable nor practicable to be objective. It is difficult to theorize on a life which one is living moment by moment. Literary theory, on the other hand, allows the outsider a means of looking at a culture he or she does not understand. Cook-Lynn believes that white people and their institutional centers of learning have coopted and poached from Native American culture and homogenized it into "symbols and metaphors which are developed in contemporary literary terms and in foreign places outside of our traditional languages and lifeways to describe who we are and where we have been" (142–43). A result of this is that "indigenous peoples are no longer in charge of what is imagined about them, and this means that they can no longer freely imagine themselves as they once were and as they might become" (143). In other words, if one wants to learn about Native American literature and life, one should consult a white "expert" at the local college campus who will locate both within cosmopolitan theoretical constructs. These scholars, according to Cook-Lynn, are more interested in relating Native American writing to the international scene than they are in studying Native America itself. Therefore, being Native American is neither credible nor important to them.

Cook-Lynn also claims that "Euro-American scholars have always been willing to forgo discussion concerning the connection between literary voice and geography and what that means to Indian nationhood" (89). No critic of Irish writing can afford to ignore the connection between voice and place. Irish writers are collectively obsessed with place and, in this respect, despite the effects of Christianity on Ireland, have much in common with Native American writers. The place which the Irish are drawn to combines the general and the particular: for example, the idea of home but also the memory of a singular fuschia bush in a corner of a field or garden. There is a strong connection in Irish writing, from the Old Irish nature poetry to the work of Seamus Heaney, between people and nature, in its broadest sense. In his biography of Samuel Beckett, James Knowlson describes the Beckett family's holidays, and how deeply those ordinary days in Greystones, County Wicklow, influenced him as an artist:

> At night, the children could hear the waves crashing against the rocks and, through the windows overlooking the harbour, see the light of the Bailey Lighthouse near Howth flashing across Dublin Bay. These sights and sounds, together with those from Foxrock, Dun Laoghaire, and the Forty-Foot, were to stay deeply etched in Beckett's memory. He always loved the Irish countryside and its mountains. The County Dublin coastline with its lighthouses, harbours, viaduct, and islands permeated his imagination and pervaded his work. The recurrent images were, to use his own word, "obsessional." (46)

Although he did not "name" place to the extent that many other Irish writers have done, the places of Beckett's childhood were located near or at the source of his creative flow. One can more readily feel and hear Ireland in Beckett than one can see it.

In Eavan Boland's memoir, *Object Lessons: The Life of the Woman and the Poet in Our Time,* we are confronted with the moment of separation from place, which is as powerful in Boland's life, if not more so, as the moment of engagement with it is for Beckett:

> One morning I was woken before dawn, dressed in a pink cardigan and skirt, put in a car, taken to an airport. I was five. My mother was with me. The light of the control tower at Collinstown Airport—it would become Dublin Airport—came through the autumn darkness. I was sick on the plane, suddenly and neatly, into the paper bag provided for the purpose. (35)

Boland is removed from Ireland, from her Irish childhood, from her feeling of belonging to a place, from the informality of youth, and removed to the Irish Embassy in London, and later to New York, because her father is a diplomat. What Boland makes clear in her memoir is the negative effect that the forced termination of an Irish childhood had on her sense of identity as a person. The triumph of *Object Lessons* is the tale of how identity is rebuilt and how this is a result of her return to Ireland as a young woman. Perhaps ironically, she regains place and belonging in suburbia. A woman/poet/mother, Boland was unwelcome in a male-dominated literary city which could not conceive of such a combination of activities. By traveling outward from the center of the city to the suburban frontier of Dundrum, which was unfinished as a unit when she moved in, Boland established her own center and started a revolution in Irish writing. Hers was an inward move—physically and spiritually—which allowed her to recapture her place. The suburb, too, was a good place to live, as it was here the "hand-to-mouth compromises between town and country" were most plainly evident (169).

Boland's accounts of her childhood outside Ireland, revealed in both her poetry and essays, have been of tremendous interest to me. All emigres, exiles, and dislocated people are confronted by the distance between where they are now and the place of childhood. We must, like Boland, fill the void. In my life, I have not found this sense of place that Boland so eloquently describes, perhaps because I have not returned to live in the country of my childhood, as she did, or I have remained closed to the possibility of belonging to America because of a kind of perverse loyalty to the place where I grew up. It is likely that I have adopted the attitude of the Irish emigrant for whom no place on earth can equal the locus of childhood. In fact, what defines Irish attachment to place so well is absence: One finds in Boland's work, in Greg Delanty's work, and in songs the plaintive voice of the exile mourning the separation from Ireland. What is ironic, of course, is the difference between yearning and fact.

Although I have felt as Boland and Delanty have felt, I have also been reminded on returning to Ireland why I was happy to leave when I did.

As I read Boland's memoir, I cast glances backward to the Black Hills, and to the moment in the forest when our path was blocked by the buffalo. What our journeys have in common are children, and this binds us with Cook-Lynn as well. What has surprised me about parenthood and made it so remarkable is the fact that, for much of the time, I have been the student and my children the teachers. From their activities, I have wondered, as Boland does, whether

> there [is] something about the repeated action—about lifting a child, clearing a dish, watching the seasons return to a tree and depart from a vista—which reveals a deeper meaning to existence and heals some of the worst abrasions of time. (*Object Lessons*, 169)

In the company of my children in the Black Hills I felt the dark clouds fade and the sun warm my tightened shoulders. I was following in their footsteps and learning about America from them. My body, the place I carry around with me, was energized by the journey across the plains of America. That simple journey—a family road trip—followed by Boland's book has affirmed for me the certainty that the acts of greatest significance in our lives are those we do for others, because these return the greatest rewards. On the longest day of the year, in the sacred Black Hills, these truths were revealed to me.

The Lakota belief that the Black Hills are the source of life reminds me of Seamus Heaney's work. In recent times, Seamus Heaney, more than any other Irish writer, has explored the deep connections between human beings and the earth. For Heaney, the *omphalos*, or navel, or "the stone that marked the centre of the world," connects both the mother and child and the human being with the earth (17). In Heaney's private myth, it is the water pump which joins people to the earth and which sustains them, physically and spiritually. The path from the human to the omphalos is also the path to the imagination:

> I always remember the pleasure I had in digging the black earth in our garden and finding, a foot below the surface, a pale seam of sand. I remember, too, men coming to sink the shaft of the pump and digging through the seam of sand down into the bronze riches of the gravel, that soon began to puddle with the spring water. The pump marked an original descent into earth, sand, gravel, water. It centered and staked the imagination, made its foundation the foundation of the *omphalos* itself. (20)

When people are removed from their sacred grounds, or when these grounds are appropriated by outsiders, the consequences are deeply felt.

It is not merely a question of economics and deeds, it is much more than this: Remove the Lakota from the Black Hills or the Irish from their fields, and you cut them off from the spiritual center which grounds them, gives them identity, and provides them with the temporal and spiritual waters, as Heaney illustrates. When the connection between place and person is violated or broken, life loses its meaning. How much time will pass before the Black Hills are returned to the Lakota? A long time, if Irish history is anything to go by. The poet Wendy Rose notes that in her Hopi culture "the very worst punishment indigenous societies can inflict, much worse than death or imprisonment, is exile or to be stigmatized by your people" (411). How deeply such words resonate in the Irish psyche.

Returning to Beckett: As a young man, he was a keen golfer, and Knowlson reveals how the landscape and vista of Carrickmines Golf Club in Dublin remained with the writer throughout his life, in a quite surprising and magical way:

> Golf was for him, he told Lawrence Harvey, "all mixed up with the imagi-
> nation," with the impact on him of the ocean, which one could see from
> the local course, and the landscape of the Dublin foothills. He knew, he
> said, "every blade of grass." At night, when he could not sleep, even many
> years later in France, he would play over and over again in his mind all the
> holes on the pretty bracken and heather course. (Knowlson, 75)

To help himself fall asleep, Beckett recalled the repeated actions of the round of golf and their singular rhythms which also functioned as entryways to the hills and the bay. Beckett brought himself back to place. While different from Boland and Heaney in seeming to resist place so much, in fact, he did no such thing.

I have resisted the Black Hills. Today, it's a tourist trap where you can see Mt. Rushmore and Crazy Horse taking shape, where you can gamble your money away in Deadwood. For many, the Black Hills mean Mt. Rushmore's triumphant faces. I have resisted, out of a fear of oversimplification, to make the all too easy connections between Irish history and Sioux history, between Wounded Knee and Vinegar Hill. It is true that they overlap; however, they are not the same and can never be honestly compared. Also, I have resisted because I do not know the history of the Black Hills well enough, and because I am unable to speak the language. Nevertheless, I did travel to the Black Hills from Nebraska, and I was a witness to their power and sacred qualities. The spirits of the hills overpowered my senses, and I emerged from their corners transformed. Of this family road trip, of sense of place, of exile, of the brilliance of Eavan Boland's vision, of the longest day, I have borne witness.

Works Cited

Index

Works Cited

CHAPTER 1. EXILE, ATTITUDE, AND THE SIN-É CAFÉ

Berkeley, Sara. *Facts about Water: New & Selected Poems.* Dublin: New Island Books, 1994.

Black 47. *Fire of Freedom.* "Rockin' the Bronx." New York: SBK Records, 1993.

Black 47. *Home of the Brave.* "American Wake." New York: SBK Records, 1994.

Boland, Rosita. "Arriving." In Dermot Bolger, ed., *Ireland in Exile: Irish Writers Abroad.* Dublin: New Island Books, 1993.

Bolger, Dermot, ed. *Ireland in Exile: Irish Writers Abroad.* Dublin: New Island Books, 1993.

Bolger, Dermot, ed. *The Journey Home.* London: Penguin, 1990.

Delanty, Greg. *Southward.* Baton Rouge: Louisiana State University Press, 1992.

Montague, John. *The Dead Kingdom.* Winston-Salem, N.C.: Wake Forest University Press, 1984.

Mulkerns, Helena. "Emigrants Catch the Bus." *Irish Times Weekend Supplement,* December 16, 1995, p. 2.

O'Connor, Joseph. Introduction to *Ireland in Exile: Irish Writers Abroad,* ed. Dermot Bolger. Dublin: New Island Books, 1993.

Rich, Adrienne. *Diving into the Wreck: Poems 1971–1972.* New York: Norton, 1973.

"Rock and Folk." *New Yorker.* February 7, 1994, p. 18.

CHAPTER 2. THE LONG JOURNEY HOME TO BROOKLYN

Bloom, Harold. *The Anxiety of Influence: A Theory of Poetry.* New York: Oxford University Press, 1973.

Bolger, Dermot. *The Journey Home.* London: Penguin, 1990.

Cisneros, Sandra. *The House on Mango Street.* New York: Vintage, 1989.

Cisneros, Sandra. *Woman Hollering Creek.* New York: Vintage, 1991.

Doyle, Roddy. *Paddy Clarke Ha Ha Ha.* New York: Viking, 1993.

Ebest, Ron. Review of *The Next Parish Over: A Collection of Irish-American Writing. Éire-Ireland* 29, no. 3 (1994): 180–82.

Ellis, Trey. "The New Black Aesthetic." *Callaloo* 12, no. 1 (1989): 233–51.

Fanning, Charles. Introduction to *Studs Lonigan,* by James T. Farrell. Urbana and Chicago: University of Illinois Press, 1993, pp. ix–xxxi.

Fanning, Charles. *The Irish Voice in America.* Lexington: University Press of Kentucky, 1990.

Fanning, Charles. "The Literary Dimension." In Lawrence J. McCaffrey et al., eds., *The Irish in Chicago.* Urbana and Chicago: University of Illinois Press, 1987, pp. 98–145.

Farrell, James T. *Studs Lonigan.* 3 vols. 1932, 1934, 1935. Reprint. Urbana and Chicago: University of Illinois Press, 1993.

Greeley, Andrew M. *That Most Distressful Nation: The Taming of the American Irish.* Chicago: Quadrangle Books, 1972.

Heaney, Seamus. *Station Island.* New York: Farrar, Straus, and Giroux, 1985.

Jenkins, Simon. *Times* (London). October 28, 1994.

Joyce, James. *A Portrait of the Artist as a Young Man.* New York: Penguin, 1964.

Kelman, James. *How Late It Was, How Late.* New York, Norton, 1995.

Lyall, Sarah. "Booker Prize Winner Defends His Language." *New York Times,* November 28, 1994, pp. B1–2.

McCaffrey, Lawrence J. *The Irish Diaspora in America.* Bloomington: Indiana University Press, 1976.

McCaffrey, Lawrence J. *Textures of Irish America.* Syracuse, N.Y.: Syracuse University Press, 1992.

McCaffrey, Lawrence J., Ellen Skerrett, Michael F. Funchion, and Charles Fanning, eds. *The Irish in Chicago.* Urbana and Chicago: University of Illinois Press, 1987.

McGonigle, Thomas. Afterword to *Season at Coole,* by Michael Stephens. Normal, Ill.: Dalkey Archive Press, 1984, pp. 172–75.

Miller, Kerby A. Review of *The Irish in Chicago,* ed. Lawrence J. McCaffery, et al. *American Historical Review* 93, no. 5 (December 1988): 1393–94.

Montague, John. *Collected Poems.* Winston-Salem, N.C.: Wake Forest University Press, 1995.

Moore, Brian. *The Lonely Passion of Judith Hearne.* Boston: Little, Brown, 1955.

O'Brien, Edna. *The Country Girls Trilogy.* New York: Plume, 1992.

Schlesinger, Arthur, Jr. *The Disuniting of America.* New York: Norton, 1992.

Smith, Dinitia. "Still Writing, Walking and Celebrating New York." *New York Times,* May 11, 1995, p. B3.

Stephens, Michael. *The Brooklyn Book of the Dead.* Normal, Ill.: Dalkey Archive Press, 1994.

Stephens, Michael. *Green Dreams: Essays under the Influence of the Irish.* Athens: University of Georgia Press, 1994.

Stephens, Michael. Interview by Mike Hudson. *Irish Echo,* March 9–15, 1994, p. 41.

Stephens, Michael. *Season at Coole.* Normal, Ill.: Dalkey Archive Press, 1984.

Wall, Eamonn. "Aidan Higgins's *Balcony of Europe:* Stephen Dedalus Hits the Road." *Colby Quarterly* 31, no. 1 (Spring 1995): 81-87.

Wall, Eamonn. Review of *The Brooklyn Book of the Dead*, by Michael Stephens. *Washington Post Book World*, March 20, 1994, p. 11.

CHAPTER 3. IMMIGRATION, TECHNOLOGY, AND SENSE OF PLACE

Hughes, Langston. *The Collected Poems of Langston Hughes*. Ed. Arnold Rampersad. New York: Knopf, 1994.
Norris, Kathleen. *Dakota: A Spiritual Geography*. New York: Ticknor and Fields, 1993.

CHAPTER 4. READING MARY GORDON'S *FINAL PAYMENTS* IN AMERICA

Bennett, Alma. *Mary Gordon*. New York: Twayne, 1996.
Carlson, Julia, ed. *Banned in Ireland: Censorship & the Irish Writer*. Athens: University of Georgia Press, 1990.
Cullinan, Elizabeth. *House of Gold*. Boston: Houghton Mifflin, 1970.
Fanning, Charles. "New York Irish Writing Since the 1960s." In Ronald H. Bayor and Timothy J. Meagher, eds., *The New York Irish*. Baltimore: Johns Hopkins University Press, 1996.
Gordon, Mary. *The Company of Women*. New York: Random House, 1980.
Gordon, Mary. *Final Payments*. New York: Random House, 1978.
Gordon, Mary. *Good Boys and Dead Girls and Other Essays*. New York: Viking Penguin, 1991.
Gordon, Mary. Interview by Sandy Asirvatham. *Poets & Writers* (July/August 1997): 50–61.
Gordon, Mary. *Men and Angels*. New York: Random House, 1985.
Gordon, Mary. *The Other Side*. New York: Viking Penguin, 1989.
Gordon, Mary. *The Rest of Life: Three Novellas*. New York: Viking Penguin, 1993.
Gordon, Mary. *The Shadow Man*. New York: Random House, 1996.
Gordon, Mary. *Temporary Shelter*. New York: Random House, 1987.
Lee, Don. "About Mary Gordon: A Profile." *Ploughshares* 23, nos. 2 & 3 (Fall 1997): 218–25.
Moore, Brian. *The Lonely Passion of Judith Hearne*. Boston: Little, Brown, 1955.
O'Brien, Edna. *The Country Girls Trilogy*. New York: Plume, 1987.

CHAPTER 6. THE SEARCH FOR MAJESTIC SHADES

Berryman, John. *The Dream Songs*. New York: Farrar, Straus, and Giroux, 1969.
Boland, Eavan. *Object Lessons: The Life of a Woman and the Poet in Our Time*. New York: Norton, 1995.

Bolger, Dermot. Foreword to *Ireland in Exile: Irish Writers Abroad,* ed. Dermot Bolger. Dublin: New Island Books, 1993, pp. 7–10.

Brown, Terence. *Ireland: A Social and Cultural History, 1922–1979.* London: Fontana, 1985.

Chapman, Patrick. *The New Pornography.* Cliffs of Moher, Co. Clare: Salmon Publishing, 1996.

Collins, Billy. *The Art of Drowning.* Pittsburgh, Pa.: University of Pittsburgh Press, 1995.

Cowley, Malcolm. *Exile's Return.* New York: Viking, 1951.

Fiacc, Padraic. *Ruined Pages: Selected Poems.* Ed. Gerald Dawe and Aodán Mac Pòilin. Belfast: Blackstaff Press, 1994.

Fitzpatrick-Simmons, Janice. *Settler.* Galway: Salmon Publishing, 1995.

Ginsberg, Allen. *Collected Poems.* New York: Harper and Row, 1984.

Gordon, Mary. *Final Payments.* New York: Random House, 1978.

Hamilton, Ian. *Robert Lowell: A Biography.* New York: Random House, 1982.

Heaney, Seamus. *Station Island.* New York: Farrar, Straus, and Giroux, 1985.

Heffernan, Michael. *The Back Road to Arcadia.* Galway: Salmon Publishing, 1994.

Howard, Ben. *Lenten Anniversaries: Poems 1982–1989.* Omaha, Nebr.: Cummington Press, 1990.

Howard, Ben. *Midcentury.* Cliffs of Moher, Co. Clare: Salmon Publishing, 1997.

Howard, Ben. *The Pressed Melodeon: Essays on Modern Irish Writing.* Brownsville, Oreg.: Story Line Press, 1996.

Kavanagh, Patrick. *Selected Poems.* Ed. Antoinette Quinn. London: Penguin, 1996.

Kearney, Richard, ed. *Across the Frontiers: Ireland in the 1990s.* Dublin: Wolfhound Press, 1988.

Kennedy, Anne. *The Dog Kubla Dreams My Life.* Galway: Salmon Publishing, 1994.

Lendennie, Jessie. *Daughter.* Galway: Salmon Publishing and Washington, D.C.: Sign Post Press, 1988.

Loomis, Sabra. *Rosetree.* Farmington, Maine: Alice James Books, 1989.

Lowell, Robert. *Day by Day.* New York: Farrar, Straus, and Giroux, 1977.

Luftig, Victor. "A Migrant Mind in a Mobile Home; Salmon Publishing in the Ireland of the 1990s." *Éire-Ireland* 36, no. 1 (Earrach-Spring 1991): 108–19.

Lynch, Thomas. *Skating with Heather Grace.* New York: Knopf, 1987.

McNulty, Ted. *On the Block.* Galway: Salmon Publishing, 1995.

McNulty, Ted. *Rough Landings.* Galway: Salmon Publishing, 1992.

Montague, John. *The Dead Kingdom.* Winston-Salem, N.C.: Wake Forest University Press, 1984.

Montague, John. *The Figure in the Cave and Other Essays.* Ed. Antoinette Quinn. Syracuse, N.Y.: Syracuse University Press, 1989.

O'Callaghan, Julie. *Edible Anecdotes.* Mountrath, Co. Laois: Dolmen Press, 1983.

O'Donnell, Mary. *Spiderwoman's Third Avenue Rhapsody.* Galway: Salmon Publishing, 1993.

Skinner, Knute. *The Cold Irish Earth, 1965–1995: New and Selected Poems of Ireland.* Cliffs of Moher, Co. Clare: Salmon Publishing, 1996.

Smith, R. T. *Trespasser.* Baton Rouge: Louisiana State University Press, 1996.

Stevens, Wallace. *Collected Poems.* New York: Knopf, 1954.

Stevens, Wallace. *Letters of Wallace Stevens.* Ed. Holly Stevens. New York: Knopf, 1966.

Tillinghast, Richard. *A Quiet Pint in Kinvara.* Galway: Salmon Publishing; Newtownlynch, Kinvara, Co. Galway: Tír Eolas, 1991.

Tillinghast, Richard. *Today in the Café Trieste.* Cliffs of Moher, Co. Clare: Salmon Publishing, 1997

Valentine, Jean. *The Under Voice: Selected Poems.* Galway: Salmon Publishing, 1995.

CHAPTER 7. HELENA MULKERNS ON THE LOWER EAST SIDE

Collins, Michael. *The Meat Eaters.* London: Jonathan Cape, 1991.

Kearns, Caledonia, ed. *Motherland: Writings by Irish American Women about Mothers and Daughters.* New York: William Morrow, 1999.

Kenny, Seán. *The Hungry Earth.* Colorado Springs: R. Rinehart, 1997.

Martin, Emer. *Breakfast in Babylon.* Boston: Mariner Books, 1997.

McDonagh, Martin. *The Beauty Queen of Leenane.* London: Heinemann, 1996.

Mulkerns, Helena. "Famine Fever." In Caledonia Kearns, ed., *Cabbage and Bones: An Anthology of Irish American Women's Fiction.* New York: Henry Holt, 1997, pp. 294–300.

O'Brien, Kate. *Mary Lavelle.* London: Virago Press, 1995.

O'Faoláin, Nuala. *Are You Somebody: The Accidental Memoir of a Dublin Woman.* New York: Henry Holt, 1998.

Smyth, Ailbhe, ed. *Wildish Things: A New Anthology of New Irish Women's Writing.* Dublin: Attic Press, 1989.

CHAPTER 8. IRISH VOICES, AMERICAN WRITING, AND GREEN CARDS

Archer, Nuala. *The Hour of Pan/amá.* Galway: Salmon Publishing, 1992.

Ebest, Ron. Review of *The Next Parish Over: A Collection of Irish American Writing. Éire-Ireland* 29, no. 3 (1994): 180–82.

Fanning, Charles. *The Irish Voice in America.* Lexington: University Press of Kentucky, 1990.

Farrell, James T. *Studs Lonigan.* Urbana and Chicago: University of Illinois Press, 1993.

Hamill, Pete. *A Drinking Life.* Boston: Little, Brown, 1994.

Joyce, James. *A Portrait of the Artist as a Young Man.* New York: Penguin, 1964.

Kennedy, William. *Billy Phelan's Greatest Game*. New York: Penguin, 1983.

Kennedy, William. *Ironweed*. New York: Viking, 1983.

Lally, Michael. *Catch My Breath*. Portland, Oreg.: Salt Lick Press, 1995

Lally, Michael. *Hollywood Magic*. Los Angeles: Little Caesar, 1982.

Liddy, James. *Collected Poems*. Omaha, Nebr.: Creighton University Press, 1995.

McCaffrey, Lawrence J. *The Irish Catholic Diaspora in America*. Washington, D.C.: Catholic University of America Press, 1984.

McEneaney, Kevin T. *The Enclosed Garden*. Orono, Maine: Northern Lights, 1991.

McGonigle, Thomas. *Going to Patchogue*. Normal, Ill.: Dalkey Archive Press, 1992.

Miller, Kerby A. *Emigrants and Exiles: Ireland and the Irish Exodus to North America*. New York: Oxford University Press, 1985.

Miller, Kerby A., and Paul Wagner. *Out of Ireland*. Washington, D.C.: Elliott & Clark Publishing, 1994.

Montague, John. *Collected Poems*. Winston-Salem, N.C.: Wake Forest University Press, 1996.

Montague, John. *The Dead Kingdom*. Winston-Salem, N.C.: Wake Forest University Press, 1984.

Montague, John. *The Rough Field*, 5th ed. Winston-Salem, N.C.: Wake Forest University Press, 1989.

Stephens, Michael. *The Brooklyn Book of the Dead*. Normal, Ill.: Dalkey Archive Press, 1994.

Stephens, Michael. *Green Dreams: Essays under the Influence of the Irish*. Athens: University of Georgia Press, 1994.

Winch, Terence. *Irish Musicians*. Washington, D.C.: O Press, 1974.

Winch, Terence. *The Great Indoors*. Brownsville, Oreg.: Story Line Press, 1995.

CHAPTER 9. ROGER BOYLAN IN HIS OWN WORDS

Boylan, Roger. *Killoyle*. Normal, Ill.: Dalkey Archive Press, 1997.

CHAPTER 10. "EVEN BETTER THAN THE REAL THING"

Barry, Sebastian. *The Engine of Owl-Light*. London: Paladin Books, 1987.

Borges, Jorge Luis. *Fictions*. London: John Calder, 1965.

Borges, Jorge Luis. *Doctor Brodie's Report*. New York: Dutton, 1978.

Deane, Seamus. "The Real Thing: Brian Moore in Disneyland." *Irish University Review* 18 (Spring 1988): 74–82.

Deane, Seamus. *A Short History of Irish Literature*. London: Hutchinson, 1986.

Eco, Umberto. *Travels in Hyperreality*. San Diego: Harcourt Brace Jovanovich, 1986.

Flood, Jeanne. *Brian Moore*. Lewisburg, Pa.: Bucknell University Press, 1974.

McCann, Colum. *Songdogs*. London: Phoenix House, 1995.

McHale, Brian. *Postmodern Fiction.* New York: Routledge, 1987.

Moore, Brian. *An Answer from Limbo.* Boston: Little, Brown, 1963.

Moore, Brian. *Black Robe.* London: Jonathan Cape, 1985.

Moore, Brian. *Catholics.* New York: Dutton, 1972.

Moore, Brian. *Cold Heaven.* London: Jonathan Cape, 1983.

Moore, Brian. *The Doctor's Wife.* New York: Farrar, Straus, and Giroux, 1976.

Moore, Brian. *The Feast of Lupercal.* Boston: Little, Brown, 1958.

Moore, Brian. *Fergus.* New York: Holt, Rinehart and Winston, 1970.

Moore, Brian. *The Great Victorian Collection.* London: Jonathan Cape, 1975.

Moore, Brian. *I Am Mary Dunne.* New York: Viking, 1968.

Moore, Brian. Interview by Eamonn Wall. In "Brian Moore, John McGahern, Aidan Higgins: An Introduction to the New Irish Fiction by Eamonn Wall." Ph.D. dissertation, City University of New York, 1992.

Moore, Brian. *The Lonely Passion of Judith Hearne.* Boston: Little, Brown, 1956.

Moore, Brian. *The Temptation of Eileen Hughes.* New York: Farrar, Straus, and Giroux, 1981

O'Donoghue, Jo. *Brian Moore: A Critical Study.* Montreal: McGill-Queen's University Press, 1991.

CHAPTER 11. HOW DECENT PEOPLE LIVE

Ellmann, Richard. *James Joyce.* Rev. ed. New York: Oxford University Press, 1993.

Higgins, Aidan. *Balcony of Europe.* London: Calder and Boyars, 1972.

Higgins, Aidan. *Langrishe, Go Down.* London: Calder and Boyars, 1966.

McGonigle, Thomas. "51 Pauses after Reading Aidan Higgins." *Review of Contemporary Fiction* 3, no. 1 (1983): 175–80.

McGonigle, Thomas. *The Corpse Dream of N. Petkov.* Normal, Ill.: Dalkey Archive Press, 1987.

McGonigle, Thomas. *Going to Patchogue.* Normal, Ill.: Dalkey Archive Press, 1992.

Stephens, Michael. *The Brooklyn Book of the Dead.* Normal, Ill.: Dalkey Archive Press, 1994.

Stephens, Michael. *Green Dreams: Essays under the Influence of the Irish.* Athens: University of Georgia Press, 1994.

Stephens, Michael. *Season at Coole.* Normal, Ill.: Dalkey Archive Press, 1984.

CHAPTER 12. THE BLACK HILLS, THE GOREY ROAD, AND *OBJECT LESSONS*

Baudelaire, Charles. "The Voyage." Trans. Charles Henri Ford. In Maynard Mack et al., eds., *The Norton Anthology of World Masterpieces.* 6th ed. New York: Norton, 1992.

Boland, Eavan. *In a Time of Violence.* New York: Norton, 1994.

Boland, Eavan. *Object Lessons: The Life of the Woman and the Poet in Our Time.* New York: Norton, 1995.

Brown, Dee. *Bury My Heart at Wounded Knee: An Indian History of the American West.* New York: Holt, Rinehart and Winston, 1970.

Cook-Lynn, Elizabeth. *Why I Can't Read Wallace Stegner and Other Essays.* Madison: University of Wisconsin Press, 1996.

Crow Dog, Mary, with Richard Erdoes. *Lakota Woman.* New York: Harper-Perennial, 1991.

Dooling, D. M. *The Sons of the Wind: The Sacred Stories of the Lakota.* San Francisco: Parabola, 1992.

Dorris, Michael. *The Broken Cord.* New York: Harper and Row, 1989.

Dugan, Kathleen Margaret. *The Vision Quest of the Plains Indians: Its Spiritual Significance.* Lewiston, N.Y.: Edwin Mellen Press, 1985.

Heaney, Seamus. *Preoccupations: Selected Prose 1968–1978.* New York: Farrar, Straus and Giroux, 1980.

Jaimes, M. Annette, ed. *The State of Native America: Genocide, Colonization, and Resistance.* Boston: South End Press, 1992.

Knowlson, James. *Damned to Fame: The Life of Samuel Beckett.* New York: Simon and Schuster, 1996.

Lazarus, Edward. *Black Hills/White Justice.* New York: HarperCollins, 1991.

Matthiessen, Peter. *In the Spirit of Crazy Horse.* New York: Viking, 1991.

McDonnell, Janet A. *The Dispossession of the American Indian, 1887–1934.* Bloomington: Indiana University Press, 1991.

Means, Russell, with Marvin J. Wolf. *Where White Men Fear to Tread: The Autobiography of Russell Means.* New York: St. Martin's Press, 1995.

"Native Peoples." Fourth World Documentation Project. 1 p. Available at http://www.halcyon.com/pub/FWDP/Resolutions/Tribal/lakota74.txt.

Norris, Kathleen. *Dakota: A Spiritual Geography.* New York: Ticknor and Fields, 1993.

Rose, Wendy. "The Great Pretenders: Further Reflections on Whiteshamanism." In M. Annette Jaimes, ed., *The State of Native America: Genocide, Colonization and Resistance.* Boston: South End Press, 1992, pp. 403–21.

Starita, Joe. *The Dull Knifes of Pine Ridge.* New York: G. P. Putnam's Sons, 1995.

Walker, James R. *Lakota Belief and Ritual.* Ed. Raymond J. DeMallie and Elaine A. Jahner. Lincoln: University of Nebraska Press, 1991.

Walker, James R. *Lakota Myth.* Ed. Elaine A. Jahner. Lincoln: University of Nebraska Press, 1983.

Index

addiction as theme, 15–16
Adrift, 107
African American influences, 11, 14, 20
AIDS, issues involving, 39–45
alienation as theme, 14–22, 121
Alvarez, Julia, 31, 32
ambivalence as theme, 5–7, 16–18
American poets in Ireland, 46–57
"American wakes," 71
An Béal Bocht (bar), 64
An Béal Bocht (O'Nolan book), 20
anger as theme, 66
Anseo (café), 11, 64
anti-Irish bias in America, 72, 74
Archer, Nuala, 9, 79, 80
assimilation issues, 14–18, 75–76
Attic Press, 63
authenticity as theme, 97–98, 118–19

Banshee, 65, 67–68
Barry, Sebastian, 91
Beckett, Samuel, 120, 123
Bell, The, 51
Berkeley, Sara, 8, 9, 79
Berryman, John, 48, 50
Black 47 (band), 11–12, 64
Black Hills, 110–18, 122–23
Blackwood, Caroline, 48
Bloom, Harold, 19
Boland, Eavan, 8, 11, 49, 121–22
Boland, Rosita, 6
Bolger, Dermot, 3, 5, 6, 16, 57
Boorman, John, 60
Borges, Jorge Luis, 46, 93
Bourke, John Francis, 62
Boylan, Roger (interview), 81–90

Breakfast in Babylon, 67
Brooklyn Book of the Dead, The, 14–22, 104
Burke, Dermot, 64

Caffery, Tom, 64
Carr, Darrah, 68
Catholicism, 33–34, 36, 72, 74
"Celtic Tiger," 13, 66
Chapman, Patrick, 49
Cisneros, Sandra, 7, 14, 20
Cliffs of Moher, 46–47
Cold Heaven, 100
Collins, Billy, 46
Collins, Michael, 67, 79
colonialism in Ireland, 71–74
Commitments, The, 27
community, sense of, 28–29
commuters, expatriates as, 3–13
Conroy, Jenny, 68
Cook-Lynn, Elizabeth, 119–20
Corpse Dream of N. Petkov, The, 104
Country Girls Trilogy, The, 16, 35
Crazy Horse, 109, 115–16, 123
Cronin, Anthony, 51
Cullinan, Elizabeth, 37, 73
cultural festivals, 64–65

Dakota: A Spiritual Geography, 29, 109
Danto, Arthur, 20
Dead Kingdom, The, 53, 76
Deane, Seamus, 95, 100
Dedalus Press, 50–51
Delanty, Greg, 8–9, 79, 121
Deloria, Jr., Vine, 119
diaspora, Irish, 3, 69